THE CENTURIES

THE CENTURIES
Portrait of a Tenement House

BY

EM JO BASSHE

The Black Heritage Library Collection

 BOOKS FOR LIBRARIES PRESS
FREEPORT, NEW YORK
1971

First Published 1927
Reprinted 1971

Reprinted from a copy in the
Fisk University Library Negro Collection

INTERNATIONAL STANDARD BOOK NUMBER:
0-8369-8878-7

LIBRARY OF CONGRESS CATALOG CARD NUMBER:
71-168508

PRINTED IN THE UNITED STATES OF AMERICA

THE CENTURIES

was first produced by the New Playwrights Theatre on Nov. 29, 1927, as the second production of their second season.

CAST OF CHARACTERS

CHAVE, an immigrant.....................{*Josephine Wehn* / *....Cecile Lifter*}
GITEE, her daughter........................*Sylvia Feningston*
YANKEL, CHAVE'S son.........................*Franchot Tone*
AN OLD IMMIGRANT..........................*Edward Robbin*
THE RABBI................................*Lawrence Bolton*
ZWI.....................................*Eduard Franz*
CHONO...................................*Samuel Schneider*
THE SHAMES (sexton of a synagogue).......*Herman Bandes*
UNCLE CHAIM...............................*Edwin Clare*
BEREL....................................*Max Leavitt*
AARON...................................*Irvin Swirdlow*
MOTKE...................................*Felix Jacoves*
DAVID...................................*Albert Gilman*
VLADISLAV................................*Lionel Ferrend*
FLOSSIE..................................*Jane Barry*
YOSHKE..................................*Herbert T. Bergman*
LOUISE..................................*Murray Franklin*
ELKE, YOSHKE'S mother.....................*Ellen Bartlett*
OLD CLOTHES MAN..........................*Nelson Frank*
REUBEN..................................*Peter Brocco*
YOUNG MAN...............................*Edwin Clare*
YOUNG WOMAN.............................*Miriam Gumble*
THE BOSS................................*Irvin Swirdlow*
THE GIRL................................*Mona Lewis*
THE MOTHER..............................*Mary Doerr*
THE DAUGHTER............................*Sheba Strunsky*
GIRL STRIKER............................*Marion Johnson*
POLICE CAPTAIN..........................*Felix Jacoves*
DETECTIVE...............................*Edward Robinson*
FIRST WOMAN.............................*Marta Proudfoot*
SECOND WOMAN............................*Mona Lewis*
THIRD WOMAN.............................*Sheba Strunsky*
FOURTH WOMAN............................*Gladys Wess*
FIFTH WOMAN.............................*Mariam Gumble*
THE HUSBAND.............................*Max Leavitt*
MASTER OF CEREMONIES.....................*Edwin Clare*

Candle Peddler, Gladys Wess; Vegetable Peddler, Felix Jacoves; Tie Peddler, Albert Gilman; Pickle Peddler, Max Leavitt; Newsboys, Nelson Frank, Jack Robinson.

Workers, pickets, strikers, immigrants, beggars, etc.: Rose Karr, Molly Bauchsbaum, Tatiana Pepper, Ora Laddon, Eleanor Olska, Ray Anderson, Madeline Ray, Polly March, Ruth Lewis, Julia Reiss.

PRODUCTION NOTES

No definite time periods or lapses are indicated
nor are seasons, months, days or hours given undue
importance since their action upon the characters
in their battle for life and existence—except in prac-
tical instances—is no different from the other phases
of their struggle. The tide and flow of their life
here is so swift, so brutal and primitive that neither
night, day, heat, cold or death can have any more
than a glancing effect upon the whole community.

* * *

SETTING: a large tenement house on the East Side
of New York and the street in front of it. The house
does not have to be in straight or flat lines but may
be broken up to form two or three small tenement
houses different in size and structural form. The
effect obtained may not be unlike that of the mudhuts
of our ancestors and may still keep within the period
of the play.

There are entrances to two basements, stairways
leading to upper flats; rear view of a section of the
house with its clothes lines and fire escapes.

The platforms used should look like flats in which

human beings actually live. Neutral platforms should be reserved for general and specific scenes and the only suggestion of their location or business in the play should be left to the actors' appearances upon them and the imagination of the audience. Thus when a scene calls for a synagogue—the Rabbi and the congregation chanting or praying designate the scene and setting.

LIGHTING: arbitrary and indirect whenever possible: the lighting in the flats should be white gas light; the reddish light of gas jets or the glow from glass shades.

ACT ONE

Program Notes:—*America* —— *Pioneers* ——
"Hole close kesh"——*Stitches, buttons, basting*——
Temple of Solomon——*Memories*——*America*——

* * * * * *

Opening Scene: *Dim light . . . an old woman
dressed in a black skirt, a white waist and kerchief
and an old man cross the stage slowly . . . their
hands are outstretched and white handkerchiefs cover
their palms . . . a plaintive female voice is singing
S. Frug's song of the pogrom period:* "Bread for
the living. Shrouds for the dead." *Early part
of evening . . . a room in an immigrant home . . .
rear: groups of immigrants asleep on chairs or floor
. . . down stage . . . a family group:*—Chave *and
her two children.*

An Immigrant Home

CHAVE

[*Wiping her eyes.*] "Bread for the living.
Shrouds for the dead." . . . They are collecting
money for the pogrom victims and here we are safe
and sound—far away from the murderers. . . .

9

GITEL

Oh, Mother, we are alive . . . we really crossed the ocean and came to America! Mother, is it really true? Is this America?

CHAVE

Yes—it is true . . . we are in America, the land of peace and freedom.

GITEL

And there is no danger? No one running after us? No drunken murderers? [*She hides her head on her mother's bosom.*]

CHAVE

Sha, don't remind me of that. . . . Sha . . . forget it . . . we are safe . . . safe at last . . . we are in America.

GITEL

Mother, I believe it was a dream . . . nothing but a terrible, frightful dream.

CHAVE

Alas—I wish it were a dream but it really happened . . . hear those voices . . . "Bread for the living. Shrouds for the dead." . . . I wish I had something to give them . . . I hope they won't wake up the Rabbi and the older people. . . . They are so tired.

GITEL

How quickly we came here! . . . I can still hear the sleighbells as we are rushing to the train. . . . Then the train and then suddenly the boat . . . it is all a part of me now . . . that was no dream . . . the ting-ting-ting of the sleighbells, the roar of the train and then the engines on the boat going pampam-pampam so gently and peacefully . . . it is in my body now . . . feel it mother . . .

CHAVE

Shake yourself dear child and then spit . . . those are not good memories . . . they are evil and should be spat out like bitter herbs taken by mistake. We must spit it all out and then forget it. We must forget.

GITEL

Who can forget the pogroms! [*A sudden quiver runs through her body.* . . .] Mother, they are running after us! Osher is being killed! Mother, Father! Help, I am being——

CHAVE

[*Embracing the girl.*] Quiet . . . quiet . . . we are far away . . . far . . . far away . . . we are in a free land. . . . [*She hums a lullaby.*]

YANKEL

She is not crying because she thinks of the pogroms. She is thinking of our home . . . America
. . . America . . . even if everything is true that
has been said about this country, what is it all com-
pared to what I have lost? It is not easy to forget
one's birthplace or boyhood chums. Can I go into
the street now and say to the boys I meet: will you
go swimming with me? Or run a race? We won't
understand each other. And they say that they even
have a different way of fighting here. I wonder what
Boruch is doing now? Or Miram or Moishe? Perhaps they've been killed in the pogrom but the soldiers were coming and I'm sure they were saved.
The soldiers will stay there a long time and there
won't be any more pogroms. I wish father would de-
cide to go back there—Mother, why can't we go back
there? . . . There won't be any more pogroms. . . .

GITEL

[*Waking up.*] No! No! We'll stay here. No,
no, no, I don't want to go back. The Czar'll take
you for a soldier, Yankel, and make you march thousands of miles and order you to kill your own
brothers and sisters and then send you to Siberia if
you refuse. Stay here and become a lawyer like you
always wanted to and become rich and then help the
pogrom victims.

YANKEL

All right I'll stay here but I'd rather go back. What's the use of being in a country where you don't know anybody?

CHAVE

We have a lot of relatives here and more landsleit than you can count in one hour . . . in fact I think most of our town came here . . . don't worry, you'll find friends, but first of all you'll have to find work.

YANKEL

Work? Must I go to work? At home I would never have worked.

GITEL

No, dead people don't have to work.

YANKEL

And what will father do? There are no synagogues here. A shames must have a synagogue— and besides, father is lazy.

CHAVE

Be quiet. The Rabbi has many disciples in America and father is out now with Uncle Chaim visiting landsleit and then they'll come here and have a meeting. Everything will come out all right.

YANKEL

This room is so crowded—not like home. How long are we going to stay here?

CHAVE

Be still . . . they are all pogrom victims like ourselves.

GITEL

Mother—how are we going to make a living?

CHAVE

It doesn't matter . . . any way at all—as long as we have peace and are safe. We'll build a new world here . . . we are safe . . . my children are safe and can be whatever their hearts desire . . . doctors . . . lawyers. . . .

GITEL

And what am I going to do? Cousin Sarah said something about working in a shop—what's a shop? She works there, too, she said, and she'll speak to the owner and——

CHAVE

Don't worry, we'll get along somehow . . . let's not bargain with fate.

YANKEL

From everything to nothing.

CHAVE

From death to life you should say, ungrateful fool.
Go to sleep. I am tired, don't trouble me, children.
[*She hums the pogrom song.*]

OLD IMMIGRANT

What is this place?

CHAVE

America.

OLD IMMIGRANT

So . . . America. . . . So. . . . Are you sure? I've
been on so many trains and ships . . . in so many
lands . . . when we came off the boat here they put
us in a wagon that had four walls and I could see
nothing and it was dark when they brought us here.

CHAVE

This is an immigrant home.

OLD IMMIGRANT

My son was going to meet me at the boat but I
didn't see him.

CHAVE

Perhaps he didn't recognize you—all fathers look
alike when they come from Europe.

OLD IMMIGRANT

They say that children here do not obey their fathers.

CHAVE

So I've heard.

OLD IMMIGRANT

I've also heard that children grow very fast here —they are full grown when they are five years old.

CHAVE

I've heard that, too, and it's a bad thing . . . a very bad thing.

OLD IMMIGRANT

I've also heard that parents obey their children here.

CHAVE

I've heard even that.

OLD IMMIGRANT

Therefore I must get ready to obey my son. [*Pause.*] My son is a rich man . . . he has ten tailors who work for him . . . ten . . .

CHAVE

Ten? Ten . . . ai, ai, ai . . . ten tailors.

OLD IMMIGRANT

Yes, ten. . . . My back is bent . . . I shall have
no trouble obeying him. The old can obey and lose
nothing. All flesh groweth old as a garment, said
Ben Siva, and an old garment is either hidden away
in the cellar or used to wipe shoes with. Ten
tailors . . . my son has ten tailors who bow to him
. . . ten . . .

ZWI

[*Comes out from some corner and shakes himself
like a dog.*] Ten tailors did you say? Ai, ai immigranten . . . immigranten . . . greenhorns! Don't
you know that there are shops that have a hundred
tailors and some even have two hundred and some
even have a thousand? . . . A thousand!

OLD IMMIGRANT

How is that possible? So many . . . ? I don't
believe it.

ZWI

Believe it or not, I'll stick to the thousand. Besides you don't have to believe in this country if you
don't want to—this isn't Europe. We've got a president here who says "Believe or not and mind your
own business."

OLD IMMIGRANT

Nu! A Jew comes out from a corner of the room
—we didn't even see him—doesn't tell us his name
and then speaks as if he has known us all his life-
time. If that's the custom of the country I am
against it. How long have you been in this country
that you know all the laws?

ZWI

Oh, I've been here two . . . two years!

OLD IMMIGRANT

Sholom Aleichem!

ZWI

Aleichem Sholom and Sholom Aleichem to you.

CHAVE

What part of Europe did you come from?

ZWI

[*Whispers.*] I ran away without a passport so it
must be a secret.

OLD IMMIGRANT

What did you do in the old country?

CHONO'S VOICE

[*From the exterior.*]   He welcomed the moon every month!

OLD IMMIGRANT

What kind of a voice is that?

ZWI

That's Chono, my partner.

OLD IMMIGRANT

A partner—in what business?   What do you do here?

CHONO'S VOICE

I do it for both of us.

ZWI

What do we do?   What . . . ?   Trouble . . . Jewish trouble . . . weddings . . . bar mitzwahs, engagements, funerals. . . .

OLD IMMIGRANT

And what is he—there—that voice—what kind of a Jew is he?

ZWI

Ah . . . ah! he is a . . . a learned man . . . he has spent his whole life at the Talmud . . . ah . . . a good man . . . a kind man. . . . Have you a little snuff . . . just a pinch . . . ? [*The* OLD IMMI-GRANT *hands him his snuff box and* ZWI *indulges himself.*] I'll take a little bit more . . . a bit more . . . for the future . . . [*Sneezes.*] You know this place is like a hotel . . . you have to pay something . . . not much . . . a little rent and you can stay here as long as you want to.

CHONO'S VOICE

We are the keepers of this place and we collect the rent.

CHAVE

[*Whispering to* OLD IMMIGRANT.] Hide your money—they are ganovim—thieves!

OLD IMMIGRANT

Truly ganovim and crazy, too! Ach!! Tfu!

ZWI

Chono, they won't pay.

CHONO'S VOICE

Ai ai! Just arrived in America and already they've dropped religion. Tell them that if they don't pay us the rent we'll starve and if we starve it'll be a sin and they'll commit the sin. [*Suddenly whistles three times.]* Zwi, some one is coming . . . Zwi! [Zwi *follows* Chono *to the street at full gallop.]*

OLD IMMIGRANT

Do you remember what you said? Truly ganovim and old men, too. Ah, if that is America . . . ah . . .
[*The* Shames, David, Berel, Chaim, Aaron *and* Motke *come in.* Uncle Chaim *acts as master of ceremonies.*]

UNCLE CHAIM

Aha, everybody asleep! Wake up! No one sleeps in America. [*Claps his hands and stamps with his feet. The* Rabbi *and the other* Immigrants *wake up.*] Rabbi, I went out and found some of our landsleit—here are a few of them. Do you remember Nison the butcher? Here he is something else but he keeps it a secret. [*As an answer the* Rabbi *grunts.*] And do you remember David the Coachman? In America he drives a double team. Drives it all by himself through the crowded streets. [*The* Rabbi *grunts again.*] And we found the man who used to sell herring at home. Here he has a fine feather and quilt store. Do you remember him? [*Pause. The* Rabbi *is silent.*] He used to sit three rows away from the door in the synagogue. Don't you remember him? [*At last the* Rabbi *gives vent to a* "Hm".] And this is Berel who used to be a

carpenter at home but here he is a rag picker—the
champion of New York.   He can find a piece of silk
in a ton of rags *AND* he is a rich man.

RABBI

[*Very amiably.*]   Sholom Aleichem. . . . Oh, yes,
I remember him . . . oh yes . . . of course. . . .

BEREL

Aleichem Sholom and let us hope that you will like
our country.

AARON

Nu OUR country!   To the rich it is always OUR
country!

RABBI

What?   Have you these abominations here too?
Cannot the tongues of these young revolutionists
ever be silenced?   They, their tongues, their sins
caused the pogroms—always speaking against the
rich, the law and God.   Why cannot these infidels
be sent to Gehenim so that the good and the faith-
ful may be free and safe?

GITEL

Rabbi, your friend the governor is not here to
carry out your wishes—we are in a free country——

RABBI

Shames! Shames!

THE SHAMES

Your servant, Reb Vellvel, is too tired to obey and besides I too am free now. [*Stares impudently at* RABBI.]

UNCLE CHAIM

Nu, nu, it is all right . . . it's the trip on the boat. . . . [*Continues as before.*] And here Rabbi is Motke Feivush who used to be the chief rubber at the sweat baths. . . . [*The* RABBI *turns away quickly . . . the landleit are displeased.*] He used to live on Mud Street not far away from the cemetery . . . you must remember him . . . you used to go to the baths yourself. . . . [*Pause.* CHAIM *scans the faces of the "landsleit."*] Rabbi in this country we are all the same and it wouldn't be right for you, a Rabbi and . . . excuse me . . . a greenhorn, to snub people.

[*The* RABBI *turns around and sullenly greets* MOTKE.]

RABBI

Sholom Aleichem.

MOTKE

[*Joyfully.*] Aleichem Sholom, Rabbi.

UNCLE CHAIM

Nu—nu fine . . . let us hear some news from Pitoshok.

MOTKE

Well . . . the news is bad.

BEREL

That's the only kind of news we expect from there.

SHAMES

We had about eight pogroms there in the last three years and if you ask me how Isaac or Tavye are getting on and I say nothing you'll know the answer yourselves. That's how things are. Nobody was safe and we didn't know if tomorrow we'd have a funeral for one or for a hundred. But we knew . . . the last pogrom . . . [*Pause.*] Well, we had to flee by sleigh and by train and when we finally got on the train we were still fleeing. That's all we could think of—run! Flee! I can still hear the Rabbi's voice: "Flee! To the cemetery! To the River! Past the mill! Flee!" [*Pause.*] There are a few souls still left there—they couldn't run and we couldn't carry them. That's all there is to the news. That's all. . . . But now that we are here what are we going to do?

MOTKE

Do? What we all do—work!

SHAMES

Work? What kind of work—how?

MOTKE

Does it matter? Work is work. Whatever comes to hand. You take a saw, go out into the streets early in the morning and somebody will give you a job.

AARON

And what do you think I ought to do?

BEREL

You—you'd make a good tailor.

AARON

I, a tailor? I?

BEREL

And why not? What's wrong with a tailor? Who's going to make your clothes if not a tailor? Everybody works here and whatever you put your hands to brings in money. If you are not ashamed of money you needn't be ashamed of doing the work that brings in the money.

MOTKE

But there are a lot of other things you can do. Rent a pushcart and peddle oranges, vegetable or halvah. Then again Jews have to have horseradish for the Sabbath—nu, you get yourself a little machine that grates the horseradish—oh, yes, they've got machines like that here—then you buy the horseradish and you're a horseradish dealer!

UNCLE CHAIM

My daughter who works in a shop has already spoken about Gitel and the boss will send over some work for her and if she does well . . . nu . . . she'll have a job. I'll tell you how my cousin Loiser made a living when he first came here: he pickled cucumbers . . . not many, but a small barrel and when they were half sour he sold them on the streets. Oh, there are lots of ways of making money here.

MOTKE

You, Reb Shlome, were used to collecting things in the old country: here you ought to do the same. Get yourself a bag and go out and buy and sell old clothes. They wear a lot of clothes here and what the rich throw away the poor wear. As you walk along the streets you shout: "Hole close cesh." You must say the last word clearly . . . like this: "Cesh."

SHAMES

I'll never learn that. Never.

BEREL

Oh, you will. All the rags and junk comes this way all the time like the tide in the ocean. We sort them out and when you become an expert you can find a piece of silk just like that! [*Snaps his fingers.*]

SHAMES

But how can I speak to people? I don't understand a word. What kind of a language have you got here? It is a strange speech when nobody understands it.

UNCLE CHAIM

Oh, there are a lot of people who understand it . . . a lot . . . I myself know a few words . . . the policeman understands it.

MOTKE

[*To* RABBI.] Don't lose heart, Rabbi . . . we'll make a collection and furnish a home for you and we'll fix up a synagogue that'll be as fine as the temple of Solomon. In fact, we already have a place rented. This will be our new Jerusalem. Now if you'll come along with me you will have a fine meal and a clean soft bed as befits a man like Reb Velvelle . . . we must go to work tomorrow. . . .

UNCLE CHAIM

Nu . . . good night to you all and have a good
night's rest. [*Exit severally with the usual part-
ings. The Shames and his family and the two old
immigrants remain.*]

SHAMES

Well, did you hear it all? But I shall be afraid
to go out tomorrow . . . there is so much to be
seen . . . so much going on . . . what noise . . .
oh, my eardrums are just bursting . . . this then is
America, the land of promise! I want to cry for
joy! We are alive! Mother! Children! You, Gitel,
and you, Yankel, must work. You are full grown
now. You cannot loaf around like you did in Europe. Here you must work, for your father is old.
The time for play is over. Tomorrow you begin.

YANKEL

Why can't we go back to our old home?

SHAMES

This is our home—we have no other home.

GITEL

I'll work . . . don't fear. . . . [*Coddling to her
mother.*] I'll work for you as well as for myself,

Mother. . . . [*Bitterly—turning to her father.*] I won't deny you my share, Father, but remember: everybody works in America and one doesn't get old at your age.

CHAVE

Sha . . . don't quarrel with your father, child, he will work too. . . .

SHAMES

Is it any business of hers if I work or not?

YANKEL

I don't want to work . . . at home I would never have worked . . . you wanted me to study, didn't you? I'll go back home by myself . . . I know the way. . . .

GITEL

Be quiet, Yankel . . . don't run away from work, like father . . . work first and then you'll find a way to study, too, like the poor students at home. Then you can go wherever you like.

SHAMES

Nu, nu, she's talking of going away again . . . Chave. . . . Why do you permit your children to talk like that? [*Pause.*] Children, have you forgotten that I am your father? Don't you think I love you? We came over here for your sake—so that you may have a safe home and a chance to grow up in a free world. I'll work too . . . tomorrow I'll begin and when we become settled you won't have to work any more. Now is that clear to you? Let us go to sleep now. I shall pray that we may have peace at last . . . peace at last. . . . [*He prays silently.*]

OLD IMMIGRANT

[*Very slowly and painfully . . . like a child lost in a forest.*] Has my son come yet? Tell him that I am waiting for him.

> [*A single gas jet illuminates the next scene:—
> a bare cold cellar. On a cot lies* VLADISLAV.]

VLADISLAV

Like a prison this place is . . . so damp and the rats are like rabbits . . . other immigrants have friends or families or countrymen but I am alone. If I could only hear someone speak a tongue that I can understand. Oh, if I had my Katia in bed with me now . . . but she is a long ways off . . . a long ways. . . . [*Softly.*] Katia . . . Katia, where are you? What are you doing? Who is with you? [*Suddenly.*] Devil take you—who are you with? Answer me! [*Gets up and flourishes his arms in the air as if beating someone.*] Take that, you slut! Now you'll be true to me! [*Falls back on cot.*]

Devils! When you are alone the devils chase you.
There was one in the room a minute ago, just as sure
as I'm alive, but it wasn't Katia. The devil is just
trying to drive me mad. If I could only hear some
dance music and dance a little or have a glass of
vodka. Dawn will never come . . . never . . . I've been
lying on this cot for days . . . perhaps this is the
country where the nights last for six months. . . .
Stepiak, the little Russian corporal who served in
Siberia, told me about that . . . tomorrow I shall
put in a complaint . . . bah you're off your head
. . . you're not in the army now . . . complaints
. . . bah . . . why did I run away from the army
to come here, eh? I might have become a corporal or
maybe a general . . . such things happen. Tomorrow I shall speak to a policeman and tell him
that I'll be a soldier again . . . I'll be a soldier.
. . . [*Pause.*] . . . one two, one two, one two left
foot right foot but he didn't have to insult me that
way . . . that officer had no right to slap me in the
face right in front of the whole regiment. I'll run
away to America I told him then and he slapped me
again and then put me in the guard house. . . .
Now I'll surely run away to America, I said . . . I
said it to myself so that he wouldn't hear me . . .
before I was fooling but now I'm going to do it . . .
and I did . . . serves him right . . . I was as honest a man as he was though he was an officer . . .

now he'll be sorry and angry too . . . one two three four five six seven . . . seven . . . seven, where is seven . . . seven?   Where is Vladislav Meschick? But Meschick isn't there . . . he ran away to America . . . here he is . . . he kept his word like he said he would . . . go and look for him . . . he'll get fifty lashes . . . fifty . . . but he won't . . . you can't touch him hahaha. . . . Who's there? Gospodi! Who are you? Meschick is not here . . . not here . . . he is going back to the army . . . leave him alone!

[FLOSSIE *saunters on.*]

FLOSSIE

Yoyohohoho look what dropped out of the sky . . . a customer in a uniform. Yoyohohoho! What a nice soldier boy. Where did you come from, my little sweat pea? Hey, don't look so sour or I'll push your face in. Say, I ain't no sour grapes and you ain't no fox. Did the reception committee and the brass band miss you, baby, or are youse just a natural born comstock? Ah, I guess I know your feelings. I felt the same when I came to this blessed country . . . but now . . . look at me . . . just look at me . . . I've still got my own hair and my own teeth . . . a pair of shoes . . . two dresses and a prescription for a cough. Whew! Say, is your mezuma in your sock or do you carry it close to your little baby heart? Not that I am interested, but a word from the wise to the stupid is worth something. Say, can't you talk at all . . . at all? Holy washday, this he-cow don't understand no more than a deaf motorman goin' top speed. Hey, Yoshke, we starve. this customer's a washout . . . a flood. . . . Has the great man Yoshke given you the glad hand yet? No? Then you ain't been introduced to America yet!

[Zwi *and* Chono *edge their way in on tiptoe.*
Flossie *runs out, shouting.*]

FLOSSIE

Yoshke, Yoshke!

ZWI

Shsh! Don't make so much noise . . . it's nobody . . . shshsh, Chono . . . an immigrant . . . another one of Yoshke's customers . . . Yoshke's net is big, he's got agents in "Kessel Garten" collecting them.

CHONO

He looks like a Pole. I'll speak to him. You speak Polish?

VLADISLAV

[*Joyfully.*] Yes, yes.

ZWI

When did you come?

VLADISLAV

This afternoon . . . they brought me here and I don't know where I am or what I'm going to do.

ZWI

Listen, you'd better get away from here or he'll hire you out to somebody and get most of the wages.

VLADISLAV

[*Going to door.*] I'll go away. But I'm afraid to leave this place . . . I don't know anybody . . . where could I go? I'll stay here better.

CHONO

[*Pushing* VLADISLAV.] Go on . . . go before Yoshke sees you, for when he gets his claws on you you'll never run away again. [YOSHKE *and* LOUIS *suddenly appear in the doorway.*]

YOSHKE

What the hell is happening here? What are you guys doing here again? Kick them out, Louis, and do it good and plenty. [LOUIS *obeys:* ZWI *and* CHONO *are put out.* YOSHKE *sizes up* VLADISLAV.] Strong fellow, ain't youse? Hey, Louis, take this polack over to Callahan's: he needs pick and shovel men. Tell him to give you a receipt and no gypping because this guy's fresh and tough. Get me?

LOUIS

All right, Yoshke. [*Motions to* VLADSILAV *and the two walk out.* YOSHKE *lights a cigar and stretches himself on the cot.* ELKE *comes in slowly and stops at the door.*]

ELKE

Yosel, Yosel,—why did you keep away from me all day? You haven't seen me in fifteen years and you did not even greet me.

YOSHKE

I'm a busy man . . . very busy . . . I've got a lot of people to take care of. . . . Well, how is the old town? Who's dead and who's stealing horses now that I'm away? So he is dead, eh?

ELKE

Your father. Yes.

YOSHKE

A hell of a father . . . may his soul rust in hell. . . . I'm sorry I wasn't there myself to see him die and laugh in his face.

ELKE

Your father was a holy man and read the Talmud every day.

YOSHKE

Well, he doesn't read it now, does he? I didn't bring you over to tell me of my father.

ELKE

Be charitable, my son.

YOSHKE

Charitable? That's a nice word . . . yes . . . I was a bad boy, wasn't I? I did a lot of bad things. I was the terror of the town. Charity—what's that mean? [*Slight pause and change of tone.*] It was never one of my good points, was it? Was it? I'm asking you that! You're afraid to answer me, aren't you? Well, you were charitable, you and he, when you dragged me from the cellar and hitched me to a horse and then drove me twenty miles. Well, remember this: *I* am *not* charitable.

ELKE

I didn't do that to you. No.

YOSHKE

A damn good excuse . . . you told the police to do it. . . . What did I do? What was it? I suppose I stole something. And then—you bound me and kept me locked in the cellar and called the police.

Didn't you keep me locked in the cellar until the police came? All because you thought I'd turn out to be a thief.

ELKE

We thought it was for your own good.

YOSHKE

Yes, good . . . it did the horse a lot of good . . . I helped him pull the wagon and I got the lashes from the policeman that he would have got. Snow. I'm being lashed. Where are we going? To jail! I'll never forget my parents, the policeman, or the horse.

ELKE

Is that why you brought me to America? Is America the judgment place for our deeds and misdeeds? Why did you bring me over here? So that you may— [*She gulps the rest of the sentence and covers her face. Pause.*] How do you make a living here?

YOSHKE

By my fist.

ELKE

Your face is all cut up.

YOSHKE

The cuts on my face brought you over here. They cost money. They own this tenement and pretty soon they'll get deeper and longer and then buy the whole damn street!

ELKE

Is this the way they live in America?

YOSHKE

That's the way *I* live in America.

ELKE

And what do you want your mother to do to earn her bread?

YOSHKE

You see this pack of letters? They are yours. In each letter you beg me to bring you over here. . . . "I am starving. . . . There is danger of another pogrom here. . . . Save your mother." . . . They are your letters?

ELKE

[*Weakly.*] Yes.

YOSHKE

I shouldn't have opened these letters . . . should have thrown them in the fire, but I brought you over here just the same . . . [*Insinuatingly—bitterly.*] and I can send you back if I want to. . . . Send you back to starve . . . as I starved when I was running from my mother's home . . . as I starved when

I came over here . . . understand me. . . . I have no pity . . . no honor . . . nothing . . . I brought you over here . . . to . . . Do you understand?

ELKE

To . . . punish me . . . I suppose.

YOSHKE

I am not like you or my father. . . . I shall give you a bed and food and money. . . .

ELKE

In return for what? Not for being your mother? What must I do?

YOSHKE

I have some girls for you to take care of. . . .

ELKE

Children?

YOSHKE

Girls. . . . Girls with lots of powder on their faces and little clothes . . . The old business!

ELKE

[*She seems to be swimming in the air . . . suddenly rushes at* YOSHKE *furiously.*] Yoshke, I curse the hour I conceived you. . . . I curse the day I gave birth to you. [*Her fingers try to cut into his body. . . . She falls back to the door.*]

YOSHKE

You don't have to do it . . . you can go back home . . . they'll send you back.

ELKE

[*In a trembling voice.*] Alter . . . my husband . . . your grave is far away from here, but I invoke your spirit to come to my aid here and now! The vengeance of a son is more terrible than all the curses in the world. [*Sinking to the ground.*] Alter, I am coming to you . . . it is better than to live . . . Alter . . . I do not hear your voice . . . you must give me an answer . . . you were wise always . . . what must I do now? What must I do?

YOSHKE

Go back to your home town . . . go back to starve . . . be eaten up by rats. . . . That's more than you deserve. . . . My father, Alter, will never speak to you while I'm here . . . his soul is too pure.

ELKE

Must I serve the devil in order to live? Must I sell my honor for the things that make life? Must I join my son in his life of shame and horror?

YOSHKE

If you're going to wait for an answer from the
dead, don't keep me waiting. I ain't got the time.
One, two, three and you're on the boat . . . they
are waiting there for you. . . . Back to the lousy
little village to starve, to be raped by Cossacks, to be
murdered in a pogrom. . . . What's your answer?

ELKE

[*Lifelessly.*] I'll serve not my son but the devil,
and if there is any punishment let it fall on my own
head, for we are born to live, and death comes only
after life, and the breath of life is still within me.

YOSHKE

He held the whip in his right hand. . . . Swish!
[*Lights: Early morning. A woman is singing:
"Abrivele der mamen Solstu nit fersamen,
etc." A peddler brings on a small barrel and
plants himself near the stairway.*]

On the Street

PICKLE KING

Pickles, half sour pickles, pickles! Pickles! Half
sour! Mmmmm taste them!
[*A man with some ties in his hand comes on
slowly.*]

TIE MAGNATE

Ties! Ties! Ties! All kinds, mostly silk! Silk ties! Nothing but silk! [*He spies* YOSHKE *peeking out of the saloon and skips off.* YOSHKE *emerges and walks directly to the pickle peddler who cringes and moves his barrel away.*]

YOSHKE

Where's your license? Heh? Where's your license?

PICKLE KING

I . . . I had one . . . I got one from you last month, don't you remember?

YOSHKE

I ain't no bookkeeper,—where's the license? Show me!

PICKLE KING

I ain't got it now, but I'll get another one as soon as I make some money. You can trust me . . . just let me stay here today and I'll fix you up.

YOSHKE

Gerrarehere before I kick youse in the face! Don't come back here until you get a license or your wife'll look for a new husband! Gerrarehere! [*The* PEDDLER *drags himself off:* YOSHKE *returns to the saloon. The* TIE MAGNATE *shuffles on.*]

TIE MAGNATE

[*Almost a whisper.*] Ties . . . ties . . . ties . . . [*But fear of* YOSHKE *forces him off again.*]
[THE SHAMES *is on the stairway, a burlap bag in his hand.* AARON *is at the foot of the stairway, a saw under his arm.*]

On the Stairs

THE SHAMES

Good morning, Aaron . . . what are you going to do?

AARON

How should I know? My cousin bought me a saw and says to me: "You'll be a carpenter." Nu, I'll be a carpenter. At home I was a student of watchmaking, here I'll be a carpenter. I'll saw. He says it is sharp . . . if it's sharp it'll cut. . . . I'll put it to the wood—push down and then pull . . . if it doesn't cut I'll know it is a bad saw.

THE SHAMES

Perhaps it'll be because you are not a carpenter?

AARON

Is it my fault that I wasn't born a carpenter? But if I can't saw, I'll hammer nails . . . anybody can do that with a hammer and nails and if I fail in that, I'll sell horseradish. I am a young man and I can learn things.

THE SHAMES

You're too late for horseradish. . . . Mayerke is already selling it.

AARON

That's what I call bad luck. . . . Nu, I'll find something else. . . . What are you doing with that bag?

THE SHAMES

I wish I knew as much about trouble as I know about this business. Motke figured it out for me. He gave me this bag and some money that I can't even count and told me to shout ten words as I walk in the street.

AARON

What are the words?

THE SHAMES

Hollclose . . . hollclose . . . did you ever hear of such crazyness? Hollclose—and there is another word which I forgot . . . it goes like this . . . mmmmmm it's a hard word . . . mmmm.

[An old clothes man walks on.]

OLD CLOTHES MAN

Old clothes cash, old clothes cash!

THE SHAMES

That's the word! That's it! "Cesh." Why is that man shouting it? Say, old man, why are you shouting the words that were given to me? My own nephew gave me those words.

OLD CLOTHES MAN

And I got those words from the inspector.

THE SHAMES

From the inspector?

....OLD CLOTHES MAN

Don't you know the inspector that lives in that saloon? [*Pointing to his badge.*] See . . . here it is written that I may use the words.

THE SHAMES

I am an immigrant and a pogrom victim and I have no other trade.

OLD CLOTHES MAN

I am an immigrant, too, and a victim of everything.

THE SHAMES

But I have a big family.

OLD CLOTHES MAN

Who hasn't? And every family eats . . . that's
the lot of the Jew: families that eat . . . old clothes
cash . . . old clothes cash . . . [*Goes off.*]

THE SHAMES

Now I shall starve . . . that man took my liveli-
hood away. . . . Is there no law in this land? I
shall have to go back to the family and tell them the
terrible news. [*He goes up to his flat.* Zwi *and*
Chono *shuffle on: the former carries a cape slung
over his arm; the latter a few books.*]

On the Street.

ZWI

A cape, a cape, a cape!

CHONO

A book, a book, a book!

ZWI

[*To* Aaron.] Good morning to you . . . how
would you like to buy a fine cape which the great
cantor Sirota once wore? I just got it from him.

AARON

I am a carpenter, what do I want a cape for?

CHONO

Nu—then buy this book for Yom Kippur.

AARON

Yom Kippur? What are you talking about—that's five months away!

ZWI

Ah, greenhorn—Yom Kippur comes earlier in this country because of the heat.

CHONO

Nu, if you don't buy this book I'll make this business with you: pay us for walking and we'll take you to a place where they need a carpenter.

AARON

That kind of business I can understand. Let us go.

[*A woman still dressed in European clothes walks on carrying a pot of beans.*]

BEAN PEDDLER

Hot beans! Hot beans! Hot beans! [Zwi *steals over and snatches a few beans out of the pot. The* PEDDLER *takes them away from him.*] Ganoff! Ganoff! Loafer!

Nu, she is beginning like Rothschild.

[*Zwi, Aaron, and Chqno march off. The Shames comes down the steps at full speed . . . stops at the foot of the stairway and shouts.*]

THE SHAMES

Holl close cesh, holl close cesh! These are MY words! Holl close cesh! This is *my bag* and these are *my words!*

[*A wizened and ragged little woman shuffles on, holding a box of candles in her hand. Yoshke stops her and examines her license, then returns to his hole.*]

CANDLE PEDDLER

Candles for the Sabbath! Candles for the Sabbath! Holy candles and matches to light them with.

THE SHAMES

Holl close cesh!

CANDLE PEDDLER

Holy candles from Jerusalem! Matches to light the candles!

THE SHAMES

Holl close cesh! [*Suddenly.*] Horseradish! I've got horseradish in my bag! Holy horseradish!

CANDLE PEDDLER

Horseradish is not holy, you infidel!

THE SHAMES

A smart woman you are—how long have you been in this country that your tongue is so free?

CANDLE PEDDLER

Never mind . . . in Russia I had a permit from the government to sell matches and candles and here I have one too. . . . I am a respectable woman and you are nothing but a greenhorn.

THE SHAMES

I am a Shames and Reb Velvelle is my Rabbi. Nu?

CANDLE PEDDLER

A shames? From the old country? And Reb Velvelle's shames, too? I am ashamed of myself . . . excuse me a thousand times . . . here's a candle for the synagogue . . . put it in a high place and light it on the Sabbath. [*Whispers.*] There's small profit in candles but as the synagogue uses a lot—we'll split the profit if you buy them from me. That's no sin. Where is your synagogue?

THE SHAMES

We haven't got the synagogue yet, but they are fixing one up.

CANDLE PEDDLER

What—no synagogue? What kind of a "shames" are you if you haven't got a synagogue? Give me back the candle—you don't need it . . . pfu on America—a shames without a synagogue . . . pfu . . . ai ai what fakers we got ai ai. [*Marches off.*] Candles . . . real holy candles . . . holy candles.

THE SHAMES

She abuses me because I haven't got a synagogue, as if it's my fault. Ah, I am tired already . . . there's no use in going out to look for business— I'll never find it anyway. [*Spreads out his bag and sits on it.*] That woman will be a millionaire some day . . . what a tongue . . . but at least I can understand her . . . she hasn't lost her tongue and speaks like a human being, not like the Goyim whose speech no one can figure out. Now what can I do with the money Motke gave me when no one comes to offer me anything to sell? At home I'd just have to whisper that I want to buy something and the whole town would be at my door in a minute. But worse than that, I can't even have the afternoon nap that I used to take at home. You can't sleep in the middle of the day, they say. A free country, bah! If we only had a synagogue I'd fix myself a nice cozy corner with a few cushions, a tea kettle by my side, and with no pogroms and no holl close cesh business to bother me—what else does a shames want of life?

[REUBEN *comes on carrying a large bundle of clothes.*]

REUBEN

Mister, where is number 64? [THE SHAMES *looks at him blankly.*] Number 64?

THE SHAMES

Nm . . . hm . . . speak your mother tongue . . . speak Jewish,—what do you want?

REUBEN

Number 64 . . . Finkel.

THE SHAMES

Finkel . . . that's my name.

REUBEN

Here's a bundle from the shop for Gitel Finkel.

THE SHAMES

My daughter . . . [*To himself.*] Nu, that means a little money for the family. I'll call her down. [*Goes up.* REUBEN *sits on the step.* GITEL *runs down, eager and happy.*]

REUBEN

Do you speak English? No? Guess I got to
make it up in Jewish then. This bundle is for you
from the shop . . . shirtwaists . . . you got to
baste them and then stitch them. You got to have
it done by tonight. If the job's good the boss'll
give you a regular job in the shop.

GITEL

What is it like, working in a shop?

REUBEN

You never worked in a shop? [GITEL *shakes her
head.*] Never? How old are you?

GITEL

Fifteen.

REUBEN

Is that the truth? Fifteen? I got my working
papers a long time ago—I don't remember how
long ago.

GITEL

Do you like working in a shirt waist factory?

REUBEN

No. Too many girls . . . they're always faint-
ing or getting their fingers caught in the machines

and the machines are enough to wake up all the dead. You see, most of them are greenhorns and they've never worked in a shop before. The bosses themselves don't know what the business is for . . . they just took a chance and opened a shop without knowing anything about running one. I'm going to quit pretty soon . . . I got my eye on a good job where I can learn something . . . a silk underwear factory . . . they make all kinds of silk underwear for men and . . . [*Hesitates.*] and other kinds too. . . .

GITEL

You mean for women, too?

REUBEN

Yes . . . all kinds . . . lots of nice colors and the materials are soft and you have to work only there—no home work . . . they won't trust you to take silk home . . . and they work only fifty-four hours a week but here we work sixty—but they're trying to organize a union . . . you know . . . to cut down the hours . . . don't say a word about it . . . my cousin Ida was in on the scheme and she got an iron pipe on her head . . . she isn't working there any more . . . got fired. Well, I got to go or I'll get fired, too. So long . . . I'll be back for the bundle . . . do a clean job of the stitching

. . . the foreman is a devil and he's got eyes as big as saucers. Good-by!

GITEL

Good-by! [*Watches* REUBEN *disappear and then carries the bundle upstairs.* THE SHAMES *and* YANKEL *come down.*]

THE SHAMES

See, see, your sister Gitel is already working. Is it clear to you? Everybody must work in America? Didn't you hear Uncle Chaim say that last night? You'll have easy work to do and you needn't cry. Go in the place and your cousin will teach you the words and when to shout them . . . he'll explain to you the different coins and what and where . . .

YANKEL

And what are you going to do?

THE SHAMES

Yankel, did you forget the commandments? Honor thy father . . . and mother. What I do is my own business. Come, let us go!

[*They walk off,* THE SHAMES *leading* YANKEL *by the hand.*

[ZWI *and* CHONO *skip on with packages of candles and go up to the new synagogue.*]

ZWI

I knew it! I knew it, I knew it! As soon as they said Reb Velvelle was here I knew that they would have a synagogue for him.

CHONO

Now we've got a place to sleep.
  [*They light the candles and arrange the benches.*]

ZWI

Ah, the Jewish god is not a bad landlord.

CHONO

Shsssh, I know it—that's why I am a Jew.

ZWI

You sleep in the middle.

CHONO

No, I'll sleep on the bench.
  [*From Right come the sounds of a group sing-ing and shouting a mild Chasidim ceremonial chant. The* RABBI *and the group seen in the first scene walk on singing . . . one or two are skipping a bit . . . one is clapping his hands, but the New World has already dimmed their fanaticism and the ceremony*

*is rather cold and the emotional display
abortive. As they enter the synagogue there
is a big shout and* UNCLE CHAIM *plants himself in the center of the room, important and
officious.]*

In the Synagogue.

UNCLE CHAIM

Rabbi and fellow members of this synagogue! At
last we have a synagogue where we can pray to our
hearts' content, as our fathers and their fathers
before them have prayed. This place cost two
hundred dollars to fix up. There is still sixty dollars due and we ask all to contribute according to
the size of the family and the pocketbook. Reb
Velvelle—for America this is like the Temple of
Solomon . . . it is your temple as well as ours and
we wish you long life and happiness.

ALL

Amen!

RABBI

We thank thee Lord Almighty, for saving us from
the hand of the murderer; we thank thee for having
given us safe passage across land and sea; for giving us shelter in this hospitable land. This is a new
world, new people, new temptations are in our way:
save your children from iniquity. We are safe here:

keep us safe here and do not let the hand of our enemy reach out to snatch our lives or happiness, for you are our protector.

> [*They dance . . . suddenly two newsboys appear, screaming.*]

NEWSBOYS

Pogrom! POGROM! POGROM!

> [*There is a sudden jolt as if the whole street had been blown up; the candles are put out; people rush from houses shouting, screaming.*]

VOICES

There's a pogrom in Russia! There's a pogrom in Russia!

> [*Newspapers fly in the air . . . the supply is exhausted. The* RABBI'S *booming voice is heard.*]

RABBI

Flee! Flee! To the cemetery! To the river! Flee! Flee! Escape! Escape! Flee!

> [*Sounds of sleigh bells ringing . . . trains rushing madly . . . the turbulent beating of engines . . . then there is a hush and the beat of a steamer's engines, like the beating of human hearts after a storm . . . now and then the boat's whistle blows as if in triumph.*]

*. . . The sound of the engines dies down
. . . the light comes on again surreptitiously
and we see the congregation in a corner,
hands uplifted . . . faces distorted . . .
then* UNCLE CHAIM's *voice coming as if from
the void . . .*]

UNCLE CHAIM

Words . . . only words . . . newsboys . . . this is
America . . . there can be no pogroms here.
    [*But they do not move.   The* RABBI's *lips
    part.*]

RABBI

Memories darken our thoughts and the shadow of
the past is always before us.   We are driven hither
and thither like a leaf before the wind . . . we take
on new customs . . . learn new tongues . . . the
rays of new suns bake our backs and we watch the
stars from new windows. . . .

TWO SEWING MACHINES

Whirrrr!   Whirrr!   [*Stop.*]   Whirrrr!

RABBI

What is that?   Machines?   On the Sabbath?   On
the Sabbath!   Is the Sabbath being broken?

GITEL'S VOICE

Mother, we must finish basting ten more.

CHAVE'S VOICE

On the Sabbath?

GITEL

The Sabbath does not give us bread.

RABBI

Is this then America?

UNCLE CHAIM

This is also America!

THE SEWING MACHINES

Whirr . . . whirrr . . . whirrrrr . . . [*faster* . . .]
Whirrrrrrrrr . . . whirrrrrrrrr . . . [*furiously until
climax*] whirrrrrr . . . whirrrrrrrrrrrrrrrrrr . . .
WHIRRRRRRRRRR . . . !

THE CURTAINS CLOSE

SECOND ACT

Half sour pickles——Passion——The Needle——
The Sanhedrin.

*   *   *   *   *   *   *

The street and the tenement have changed: there
is a hum and a bustle, sound and movement, some-
times rhythmical and sometimes discordant.

There are several places of business: a grocery,
a feather and quilt store; a remnant emporium, a
hole in the wall candy store with an antiquated little
soda fountain. They are not distinct establish-
ments, however, but are combined with bedrooms,
parlors and kitchens; for the process of distilling
life here is dynamic, brutal, vicious and no accounts
are taken of propriety, privacy or human needs.
Here you are sold and resold before your shoes are
laced; the market has its listings, its bears and
wolves, its kings and magnates: you must keep your
eyes open, ears cocked and fingers ready or the liquor
will flow over.

Street peddlers—a few ties . . . a half dozen
handkerchiefs—are lounging about . . . leaning
against walls or balustrades, waiting for customers;
pushcarts containing vegetables or hardware that

60

has been thrown out of regular stores as "seconds"
are wheeled about from place to place, the PEDDLERS
always on guard for the ever present meddling LOUIS
and YOSHKE.

On the Street

VEGETABLE PEDDLER	TIE MAGNATE	PICKLE KING
Schav — real home schav! Onions three pound for ten cents!	Ties silk silk nothing but silk feel it put a match to it! Silk!	P i c k l e s half sour Half sour pickles Pickled apples Pickles! H a l f sour! M m m m taste them!

ELKE

[*Pantomimes and speaks.*]   Girls!   Beautiful
girls!   Have a good time!   Girls!   Come right in!

VOICE FROM REMNANT EMPORIUM	YANKEL
Remnants! All kinds all sizes! Big enough for a dress, Missus! Small enough for the baby!	Handkerchiefs two for a nickel! Handkerchiefs two for a nickel! Pure linen! Linen two for a nickel!

LOUIS

[*To a* PEDDLER.] Move along!
[*The* PEDDLER *moves to the other side of the
street—*LOUIS *watching his movements.*]

VEGETABLE PEDDLER

This way, Missus, this way—cucumbers! I've got fresh stuff right from the market. *His* stuff is as old as Jerusalem and that's not jealousy!

COMPETITOR'S VOICE

Cucumbers! He's a liar, Missus — a liar! Come here and smell these vegetables yourself and see if they aren't fresh!

ELKE

[*Whispering to a young man.*] Come inside . . . beautiful girls . . . many of them. . . .

LOUIS

[*To a* PEDDLER.] How many times do I have to tell you to keep off this street?

PEDDLER

All right, Moiphy, I'll move along . . . I'll move along . . . anything you say.

PICKLE KING

Hey, Nachman, look at my stock!

VEGETABLE PEDDLER

Nu, nu, what's the matter with it?

PICKLE KING

Nothing the matter with it—it doesn't sell that's what's the matter! I've got four small barrels and one big one and business is rotten. I hope to hear the same from you. I'll lose a dollar sixty cents if I don't sell the whole stock! Pickles! Half sour, half sour pickles, half sour pickles, half sour pickles! Hey, Nachman, I'll sell you this business for ten dollars!

VEGETABLE PEDDLER

Go smoke a herring, I got troubles of my own. This way, ladies! This way! I am honest but I am poor, sang the prophet Elijah!

TIE MAGNATE

Bah! Look who's honest! If I trusted you with a button . . . here you are, mister, real pure silk ties—they sell them in the big stores for two dollars —here you get them for fifteen cents . . . take them for a dime!

VEGETABLE PEDDLER

Going down . . . schav . . . fresh home schav . . . only a pound left . . . here, missus, I've got

more than a pound—come here I made a mistake!
Here . . . here!

COMPETITOR

Here, Missus, I've got it . . . I've got a whole
pushcart full . . . he's got the leavings! Dirty and
only a pound!

VEGETABLE PEDDLER

Now I lose a customer by my own foolishness
. . . I've got a whole pushcart and I say I've only
got a pound! Oh, what a head I've got! But I'll
show you . . . you . . . [*He slings a bunch of
radishes at his competitor. Turmoil.* LOUIS *does
his duty.*]

LOUIS

Stop it now! This ain't no place to fight! Jesus,
where are your mothers to watch youse?

VEGETABLE PEDDLER

I'll knock his head off, the loafer! May smoke
eat up your father and his father and his father
before him until eternity!

LOUIS

Let me see your license! [THE PEDDLER *produces
his license.*] Hey what's this? This ain't for vegetables—it's for fruit. Where'd you get the license?

VEGETABLE PEDDLER

From the big inspector: Yoshke Shtarker.

LOUIS

Let's go to Yoshke's then.

[*General excitement. The peddler s shout, scream and try to rescue the* VEGETABLE PEDDLER. LOUIS *holds on to his man and they slowly move to* YOSHKE'S *saloon. The remaining peddlers take advantage of the forced absence of their competitors and, jumping like frogs in the attempt to corner a customer, furtively appropriate a bunch of carrots, handfuls of peas or a piece of velvet.* YANKEL *snatches a few apples and pockets them.* YOSHKE'S *saloon is being stormed—* LOUIS *is doing his best to shove the screaming, fighting crowd back. The swinging doors of the saloon open and* YOSHKE *emerges: immediate silence: the crowd moves back helter-skelter.* LOUIS *hands* YOSHKE *the license. He scrutinizes it but being a politician he has difficulty in making out the contents and so looks questioningly at* LOUIS.]

LOUIS

This license is for fruit and this guy is selling vegetables.

YOSHKE

[*Without a quiver.*] Five dollars for a new license.

LOUIS

Did you hear what the inspector said?

VEGETABLE PEDDLER

Another one? *I* got to have another one? Why?

LOUIS

Because this license is no good.

VEGETABLE PEDDLER

Why no good? I paid five dollars for it last week and now it's no good. I didn't make five dollars in the whole last week and now he says the license is no good. Why?

LOUIS

You can't peddle with this license and that's all there is to it.

VEGETABLE PEDDLER

How am I going to peddle then? How am I going to live?

LOUIS

I don't know—ask the Inspector. [*He looks at* YOSHKE. *No action.*] You heard what the Inspector said.

VEGETABLE PEDDLER

Inspector he calls that? Where did he come from? What does he want from my life? Oi, Columbus, Columbus!

PICKLE KING

You're like the robbers in Russia . . . always asking for money . . . money. . . .

VEGETABLE PEDDLER

Graft! Graft! Grafter!

VOICES

Graft! Graft! Grafter!

YOSHKE

[*Master of the situation.*] Get that son of a bitch and bring him in here.
[LOUIS *gets hold of the* VEGETABLE PEDDLER *and leads him into the saloon.*]

VEGETABLE PEDDLER

[*Turning to the peddlers.*] Come on to the park! We'll hold a protest meeting.

Protest meeting! Down with the grafters!

YOSHKE

[*In his best oratorical style.*] A protest meeting? Think this is Russia? This is a free country
—you don't have to protest here! How much would
a license cost you there? In fact, you wouldn't get
one at all! If you hold a protest meeting and it gets
into the papers you'll never peddle on this street
again. D'you get me?!!
    [*A few men separate themselves from the crowd
    and go left while the rest of the crowd moves
    silently to the right. The few remaining
    peddlers, finding few customers and suspi-
    cious of* Louis's *catlike movements, sidle off.*]

                                    In the Saloon
FLOSSIE

Yoshke, these people has got to understand what
this country is all about and you've got to make 'em
do it. Gimme another rye, Jack! Tell them they
can be presidents, but they got to join and vote.

YOSHKE

But they ain't citizens!

FLOSSIE

What the hell does that matter? A vote's a vote. They can belong to any damn country they please all the year around but they got to be citizens on election day. And you ought to make 'em citizens for that day, too. They got to do something for this country.

LOUIS

Sure, this pushcart business ain't gonna make you no millionaire.

FLOSSIE

There's an election coming soon. Maybe an alderman's job. Gravy and a big chest, huh?

YOSHKE

Them Ikeys would never vote for me.

FLOSSIE

What the hell they got to with it? Ain't you the boss here? But its best to be on their good side, especially the whiskers. Me old sweetie, Mac, worked it right. Always gave 'em a big affair and made 'em pay for it.

YOSHKE

That's a good idea, hey, Louis?

FLOSSIE

Mac used to collect two bucks from the corner guys . . . five from the pushcarts . . . eight from the wagons, and ten from the storekeepers. That used to do the trick.—That and a gat in your hand'll win any election.

LOUIS

Jesus, if that's the case, you're as good as elected. [*Pause.*] Say, has an alderman got to be honest?
[FLOSSIE *laughs.*]

YOSHKE

Say, Louis, start the ball arolling . . . start the collection. Go on, Louis!
[LOUIS *rushes out and stops before the candy store.*]

In the Candy Store

LOUIS

Ten dollars.

CHAVE

What for?

LOUIS

Campaign funds! Yoshke's running for alderman.

CHAVE

Ha?

LOUIS

Come on, come on, or I'll wreck this place.

CHAVE

[*Handing him bill.*] Here—that's all I got. Don't you come back again, you grafter, tramp, loafer!
[Louis *runs off.*]

In Quilt Store

WOMAN'S VOICE

[*Somewhere behind the quilts and feathers.*] I am telling you they are goose feathers . . . feel it . . . one price . . . one . . . come back . . . here . . . look . . . it's stuffed with goose feathers I am telling you . . . no. No, one price . . . one . . . one. . . . Hymie, are you practicing? . . . You want to be a loafer maybe, or a gangster like Yoshke? You should better eat poison first. You better practice some more. Practice, you hear me? Then you'll be a great man like Kreisler or Heifetz. Practice some more. . . . [*Simple scales are heard being played on a violin.*] You should have at least ten pounds for two pillows . . . at least . . . no, no, one price . . . I got to make a living too . . . not a penny off . . . no . . . no. . . .

In the Street
[*A young couple—"coney lemels"—the type
that had to be guided to these shores by elder
people . . . the type that made good picking
for the sweatshops . . . in short, a couple of
wooden Indians sans the feathers and the loin
cloth, drag themselves on, happy as two red-
birds at the approach of the mating season.*]

YOUNG MAN

It must be here . . . he said: "Go until you see
a house with steps" . . . here is a house with steps
. . . "Then you turn to the right . . . [*Accom-
plishes the difficult task.*] "then" . . .

YOUNG WOMAN

And then?

YOUNG MAN

"Then" . . . I forgot . . .

YOUNG WOMAN

A head you got, Max? A cabbage you got? Now
you count four steps.

YOUNG MAN

That's right . . . a blessing on your head . . .
four steps . . . [*He goes through the ordeal without a sign of pain and finds himself in front of the
candy store.*]

YOUNG WOMAN

But I don't see a fountain.

YOUNG MAN

What do you want a fountain for? Tzores, it is not a fountain . . . [*They enter the little candy store.*] Is this a fountain?

In Candy Store

CHAVE

[*The mark of the East Side is upon her . . . she looks tired and forlorn and her speech is tinged with a bitter humor.*] A fountain we got here he asks me! A candy store we got here. Are you a landsman too? Everybody is a landsman these days. Ah America . . . what trouble you got, please?

YOUNG MAN

It's all right . . . we haven't got trouble . . . they said there was a young man here—maybe he is your husband—who writes letters. The girl I keep company with and I want to write a letter to her parents to tell them that we— [*The* YOUNG WOMAN *nudges him in the ribs.*] Where is he?

CHAVE

My husband he is and a young man he is not . . . letters he can write because he was a teacher and a shames in the old country, but as everybody here knows everything there's nobody to teach, and as he was lazy in the old country, so is he lazy here, so he writes letters and makes no mistakes.

YOUNG WOMAN

But where is he?

CHAVE

If you're in a hurry he's not in. In the corner there on the bottles he's asleep. Kick him, not too hard, and he'll wake up.

YOUNG MAN

Kick him? What kind of a letter writer is he if you have to kick him to write a letter? In the old country we didn't kick our letter writers and educated people.

CHAVE

But we don't come from the same part of the world.—All right, here's a glass of water, throw it in his face and if he doesn't wake up you'll know that he doesn't want to write the letter and you'll have to learn to write it yourself.

YOUNG WOMAN

How can we learn to write a letter? Let's go home Max, I don't like this place.

CHAVE

Wake up, Shlome, they're going away.

THE SHAMES

[*In a sleepy voice.*] If you'll give me some seltzer and syrup mixed, I'll write the letter.

CHAVE

Hurrah for Columbus, he wakes up! A sweet throat you got. . . . A husband I got with a sweet throat. . . . Write that letter!

THE SHAMES

How anybody can write with a dry throat I don't know. Nu, if I must, I must. [*In a peremptory manner.*] Fifteen cents for two pages and you buy the paper here.

YOUNG MAN

Fifteen cents? How do you know I'll write two pages?

THE SHAMES

I'll write it, not you.

YOUNG WOMAN

For fifteen cents we don't want a letter—ten cents we'll give you.

THE SHAMES

For ten cents I'll write the Russian address there and the return address here.

YOUNG MAN

Ten cents—we're not rich.

YOUNG WOMAN

We have to sweat a whole hour before we make fifteen cents.

CHAVE

He didn't get his education for ten cents.

YOUNG WOMAN

Let's go. [*Walks towards the door.*] Ten cents, not a penny more.

CHAVE

Oh, go to Gehenim!

YOUNG MAN

Go to Gehenim yourself—ten cents!

CHAVE

Break a leg, fifteen cents.

YOUNG MAN

[*In a desperate tone.*] Nu, write that letter—the five cents is not going to make us rich or poor.
[*Writing materials are produced.*]

Begin.

YOUNG MAN

Tell them the letter is from me . . . that I am all right . . . I work in a shop making shirt waists . . . I live with Chae Dvorshe and I hope to hear from them the same . . . and now . . .

THE SHAMES

[*Imitating him.*]   And now . . . nu . . . nu?

YOUNG WOMAN

And now he wants to tell them that I am working in the same shop with him, that he is keeping company with me and that we're going to be engaged and then we're going to wait and then we'll get married.

CHAVE

[*Disgusted.*]   The man that called this country America is a loafer—this is a crazy house. . . . Look, Shlome, who's going to marry who . . . where do you come from anyway—from the wilderness?

YOUNG MAN

Not from the wilderness but from Eloshinki and it's as good a town as you came from . . . they had pogroms there as big as in any town.

THE SHAMES

But the lord spared you . . . nu, nu, even the lord makes mistakes.

YOUNG WOMAN

Did you hear that, Max? How can he be trusted to write an important letter when he talks like that? Let's go.

CHAVE

Pay for the paper first . . . pay for the paper!

YOUNG MAN

We'll never come back here . . . never!

CHAVE

Pay for the paper . . . [*Holds on to his coat.*]

THE SHAMES

Let them go to perdition and roast themselves yellow and green!

CHAVE

Pay for the paper. [*The* YOUNG WOMAN *drags her man out and they march off, indignant.*] A fine business man you are. Spoiled a whole sheet of paper!

THE SHAMES

They'll come back yet. . . .

CHAVE

I wish you'd go as they went. . . .

THE SHAMES

Ai, Chave, how you've changed . . . your face
that used to smile like a sunflower is as sour as a
pickle now . . . ah America has changed you and
who knows what'll happen to me now?

CHAVE

And you? You're ten times as lazy as you used
to be . . . you sleep day and night and your children have to work in shops to give you bread . . .
your children will never forget this . . . never. . . .

THE SHAMES

What can I do? How can I make a living? The
shames business brings in a half dozen candles and
a glass of wine on Friday night . . . that's all.

CHAVE

Yes—it's a poor synagogue—nothing to steal.
What about the holl close business?

THE SHAMES

Business she calls it! I buy and buy and buy,
and never sell, and even what I buy is no good . . .

my eyes aren't as good as Berel's . . . he's a born rag picker and I'm a born servant of the synagogue . . . but give me a chance . . . I'll talk to one of the trustees of the synagogue and we'll see . . . just let me get my afternoon nap.

CHAVE

Sleep . . . sweet dreams to you . . . as sweet as my heart. . . .

[THE SHAMES *goes to the corner again.*]

WOMAN'S VOICE

[*From feather and quilt store.*] Goose feathers! Yes! That's just what they are! You've been here two hours and you don't believe they are goose feathers yet. If you buy something I'll die from apoplexy at the surprise!

CHAVE

At home I had some honor . . . the wife of a shames . . . I had a place of honor in the synagogue and I was respected . . . here I am the wife of a loafer and my children have to work in shops . . . on the street. . . .

[*Somewhere a* WOMAN *is singing*]:

WOMAN'S VOICE

"Aufn pripetchok brent a feieril
Und in shtub is heiss," etc.

[CHAVE *joins in, shaking her head to and fro. Suddenly* YANKEL *runs in. He carries a package under his arm.*]

YANKEL

Look what I found, Mother. . . . [*Unwraps package which contains a silver tray.*]

CHAVE

You found it? How did you find it?

YANKEL

Peddling wasn't going so well so the boys went to another corner . . . so we saw something . . . so we picked it up. . . .

CHAVE

Are you sure you found it?

YANKEL

Sure . . . what do you think . . . sure . . . . . . found it. . . .

CHAVE

Shlome . . . wake up Shlome . . . !

THE SHAMES

What is it now?

CHAVE

Come here.

THE SHAMES

What are you doing here now?

CHAVE

He says he found this. . . .

THE SHAMES

Found it? You're a good finder . . . hmmmmm
. . . this is silver . . . it's worth money.

CHAVE

What kind of a father are you, when you don't
ask the boy where and how and when he found it?
Maybe he did a thing he shouldn't do it . . . ask
him. . . .

THE SHAMES

You want me to make a liar out of my son? He
says he found . . . he found it. I'll put it away
in the closet. . . . [*Does so.*] Yankel, go back and
peddle and don't let your mother make a liar out
of you . . . [YANKEL *is about to go out.*] and if
you know where to find some more of it . . . you
can keep half the money that it'll bring. . . .

CHAVE

What's this . . . what are you telling the
boy . . . ?

THE SHAMES

The boy is no fool and he knows more than you
or I . . . go ahead Yankel . . . listen only to
me. . . .

[YANKEL *goes out.*]

YANKEL

Needle threaders, needle threaders!

CHAVE

[*Tearing parcel out of* THE SHAMES's *hand, puts
it in closet.*] That package is going to be there
until I found out where he found it.

THE SHAMES

Did I say I was going to take it out? I did not.
I'm just going to . . . [*He purrs a bit . . . moves
around in a circle, then stealthily brushes against
the closet when* CHAVE *lets out a yell.*]

CHAVE

Keep away from there I am telling you.

THE SHAMES

Tfu, tfu, tfu, on you and all the devils and evil
doers. My heart jumped out of me. What did I
do that you had to yell?

CHAVE

If you go near that closet again I'll run out on the street and yell.

THE SHAMES

Yell your head off, I'm going to take it out and see how much it's worth. [*Takes the tray out.*] Nu, why didn't you yell?

CHAVE

This is the beginning of trouble . . . I don't like it . . . throw it out, Shlome. . . . [*She reaches out for the tray and begins struggling with* THE SHAMES *for it when they are interrupted by the entrance of* BEREL.]

BEREL

Hello, landsleit! Hello!

CHAVE AND THE SHAMES

Hello, hello!

CHAVE

How are you? Your wife? Your children?

BEREL

Everybody is alive and doing fine, especially my eldest daughter . . . she's growing like a flower.

THE SHAMES

Ah, you talk like a father who is looking for a husband for his daughter. Ha, ha!

BEREL

Nu, maybe you're right, but the young man isn't born yet who's worth my daughter. And how are you?

CHAVE

He sleeps . . . the children work . . . and I wait for them.

BEREL

And the business?

CHAVE

Business you call it? I wish it on the devil . . . on the devil such a business I wish . . . how is your business?

BEREL

If I wanted it better, it couldn't be better. I've got eighteen rag pickers now and pretty soon I'll need more. If I have to admit the truth, I'll say that I am making money and that I'll be a rich man soon. Well, what's America for? That's what we came here for, didn't we?

CHAVE

What did *WE* come here for? What for . . . ? We *had* to come. . . .

THE SHAMES

We weren't made to be rich so let's not hope for that. . . .

CHAVE

You good for nothing . . . why not?

BEREL

What's there to stop you from becoming rich?

THE SHAMES

Money.

BEREL

You're a more educated man than I am, but you have to work hard. . . .

CHAVE

He work hard?

BEREL

Well, if he works hard now, he won't have to work hard later on. When I first came here I worked all day and until late at night . . . in mountains of rags. My mouth and nose would be full of dirt and dust and there were more threads on my head than hair and I would have to use a fine comb to get them out. But now I won't even touch a rag. I just watch, and if I see a piece of silk or velvet . . . Nu, I'd better go . . . ! We are thinking of

moving up . . . uptown . . . yes . . . it's a cleaner
and finer neighborhood . . . you know, the children . . . I don't care. My daughter you know is a
regular Miss now. . . . By the way, I'd like to in-
vite your son to come to my house some night . . .
the children play on the piano and dance . . . tell
him to come up . . . I am not a stingy man when
it comes to dowry . . . yes? Here's my daughter's
picture. You may keep it. Good night!

CHAVE AND THE SHAMES

Good night.

[BEREL *goes out.*]

CHAVE

I want to ask you just one thing: did you in all
your life see a girl as homely as Berel's daughter?
Her figure . . . nu . . . I forgive her that, but
her face . . . never!

THE SHAMES

But he's got money and the dowry will cover her
blemishes. She'll make a good wife.

CHAVE

Yes, sell your son for a dowry. Berel buys rags
and becomes rich, now he wants to buy a son-in-law.
Give me the tray! A dishonest man you should become in your old age—you should die first!

THE SHAMES

Shsssh . . . there come the "Coney Lemels" again.

[*The couple is trying to find the candy store again.*]

YOUNG MAN

It was here but I don't see it any more.

YOUNG WOMAN

Here it is . . . ! We want the letter written!

CHAVE

We don't write letters any more.

YOUNG MAN

We'll pay for the paper.

CHAVE

All right, come in and no monkey business.

THE SHAMES

You're going to be married soon?

YOUNG MAN

Yes.

THE SHAMES

Well, here is something for you to start house-keeping with. [*Shows them tray.*]

YOUNG WOMAN

It looks like silver.

THE SHAMES

That's the only kind we got.

YOUNG MAN

But how should silver come to a candy store?

THE SHAMES

Did I ask you if you had a passport? Did I say to you your nose is too long? If you want it, you can have it for five dollars.

CHAVE

Let him have it for two dollars . . . for one dollar. Get rid of it . . . get rid of it!

YOUNG WOMAN

For one dollar we'll take it.

THE SHAMES

Nu, she mixed in, let it be one dollar. . . .

YOUNG MAN

I've got the whole letter in my head now.

THE SHAMES

Begin.

YOUNG MAN

[*Dictating.*] We are all right and hope to hear the same from you. We work in a big shop . . . we are engaged and we'll soon be married. Send us your blessings. We'll send you a picture of ourselves soon. We are making money and are happier than we were at home. That's all.

YOUNG WOMAN

We've got to go back to work now. Two machines waiting for us, like cows to be milked.

CHAVE

My daughter also works in a shop.

YOUNG MAN

In a big shop like ours, too? Ours is a very big place. But the people are lazy, not like us. We like to work in a shop, don't we, Faige?

YOUNG WOMAN

Yes, I like it, because I am not lazy like the others. They want the windows open so that they can look outside. At home I used to milk cows, but here I make a lot of money. I never thought so many people could work in one place.

YOUNG MAN

The boss is in an office where he gets the orders
which we fill. We never see the office, but that's
the head of the place. The foreman, who talks only
to us because he says we are the best workers, told
us that if not for the office, we wouldn't have work.

YOUNG WOMAN

Don't talk so much, Max, let's go to work.
Good-by!

YOUNG MAN

Good-by and when we want another letter written we'll come back.

[*They walk out arm in arm, the precious letter
in his hand.*]

CHAVE

Cow milkers making shirtwaists . . . nu let it be
. . . but as for you, be a poor Shames, but you're
not going to become another Yoshke Shtarker. One
is enough. Yankel is learning too much from
Yoshke anyway. That's all he does is talk to that
gangster. Now you're helping him out. An ortho-
dox man like you, teaching his son to be a thief.
Oi, America!

THE SHAMES

There's plenty for everybody—why should we be
cheated . . . ? Hmmmmm, I'm sleepy.

CHAVE

Sleep. . . . If you are to become the father of a thief, let it be your last sleep. . . . Your daughter is not sleeping now . . . her little fingers are sewing . . . pushing cloth under the needle and they won't open the windows because she may look out and see the sky. . . . All night long she dreams of those machines . . . the machines. . . .

THE MACHINES

Whirrrrrrr . . . whirrrrrrr . . . whirrrrrrr . . .

CHAVE

Her fingers clutch the sheets and pull them back and forth and her breath makes noises like the machines. . . .

THE MACHINES

Whirrrrrrr . . . whirrrrrrr . . . whirrrrrrr . . .

In the Factory

[*On a high platform up stage a coatless man is standing at a desk. He is holding a batch of papers in his hand. . . . A girl stands beside him . . . there is a feverish activity about him . . . he is always gasping for breath . . . the machines seem to spur him on . . . to whip him into renewed activity as soon as he relaxes.*]

THE MACHINES

Whirrrrrrr . . . whirrrrrrr . . . whirrrrrrr . . .

THE BOSS

Sixty gross size nine to Flint credit ok. . . .

THE GIRL

Ship before March Fourteen. . . .

THE BOSS

Ship before March Fourteen ninety gross size eight mixed colors Philadelphia balance of order as of January second. . . .

THE GIRL

Ship by express to arrive not later than March twelve marked. . . .

THE BOSS

Forty to Boston size seven again . . . two hundred eighty Chicago assorted sizes blue and pinks . . . credit doubtful. . . .

THE GIRL

One hundred forty to St. Paul. . . .

THE MACHINES

Whirrrr . . . whirrrrrr . . . whirrrrrrrrrr

THE BOSS

We ain't got it . . . got to hurry . . . the season starts soon . . . we ain't got it . . . better rush it . . . rush it. . . . [*From the shop comes a crash . . . the machines stop . . . women scream . . . the machines go on again.*] What's that? Hope the machines ain't broke again! Find out . . . !

THE GIRL

[*Shouting into telephone.*] What's happened? [*Pause—to Boss.*] Machine needle breaks stitcher's finger on machine sixteen!

THE BOSS

Order three gross steel needles . . . be sure it's steel . . . don't break so fast . . . thirty gross blues mixed sizes seven nine ten Rochester FOB tell foreman to hire ten more stitchers tomorrow . . . funny they don't order greens . . . lot of greens on hand . . . ship two gross greens with every consignment order.

THE MACHINES

Whirrrrr . . . whirrrrr . . . whirrrrrr . . . [*interval.*] whirrrr . . . whirrrrrrrrrrrrrrr.
[*Phone rings violently. GIRL answers.*]

THE GIRL

Jobbers' outlet wants three thousand export delivery February.

THE BOSS

Tell foreman hire twenty operators.

THE GIRL

No more room!

THE BOSS

Squeeze them in near the door!

THE GIRL

Shuts the fire exit!

THE BOSS

That's six thousand stock four green!

THE GIRL

Our order annual shipment four hundred Richmond Yellows.

THE BOSS

Wire: "Sorry no yellows stop order wire collect substitution stop bank draft ten per cent required tight market . . . signed." . . . Miss . . . we ship to old customers only . . . too many orders . . . tell him to hire five more finishers . . . [THE GIRL *protests.*]   Get a first aid cabinet . . . big one

. . . seventy to Michigan Emporium . . . sixty days . . . two per cent off. . . . Have you got the emergency 'phone numbers for the police, ambulance and fire department handy . . . ?

THE GIRL

In front of me.

THE BOSS

Always have it before your eyes . . . we are going very fast; must be prepared . . . prepared. . . . *[The machines drive him on . . . on . . . his breath . . . words . . . gestures become choppy . . . the machines crescendo . . .* THE Boss *and the machines run pace in pace until . . .]*

THE MACHINES	THE BOSS
Whirrrr *[Stop.]* Whrrrr	Four gross six eighty pinks.
. . . w h i r r r *[Stop.]*	Yellows . . . sevens . . . sixteen.
whirrrr . . . whirrrr	Mixed St. Louis Newburg nine credit.
WHIRRRRRRRRR	FOB Express wire signed COD draft.
WHIRRRRRRRR	Jobbers RUSH, rush
WHIRRRRRRRR	Rush RUSH RUSH!!!

[The shop gong rings furiously and the machines stop abruptly . . . we see the workers

homeward bound . . . tired . . . sweaty . . .
impotent. . . . REUBEN *and* GITEL *walk side*
by side . . . stop at the candy store.]

On the Street

REUBEN

It's funny to end a day with a bell . . . it seems
like a funeral. . . .

GITEL

It is like being covered with sand after lightning
strikes you. . . . We could go on working . . . on
and on . . . for the machines are lullabys that keep
you awake and rock you to sleep . . . go on working for ever . . . needles in fingers . . . dust, grit,
smoke and all, but the bell is a hundred little needles
. . . your fingers come off, you fly with the smoke.
. . . [*Suddenly.*] Go home! Go to your mother!
Go on! Hide yourself from me! [*Pushes him
away.*] Isn't it enough that I have to pull bits of
steel out of my own body . . . your eyes dance and
laugh . . . you are used to it . . . you are all steel
. . . I am being born . . . I am coming to life.
Your body is dry like the wheel that turns and
turns. . . .

THE MACHINES

[*Softly.*] Whirrrrr . . . whirrrrrrr.
[*The gong rings again. She begins to spin*

. . . REUBEN catches her in his arms; bewildered . . . uncertain as to his next step.]

REUBEN

The machines have stopped . . . don't you hear the bell . . . come . . . we are going home . . . a little slower . . . slower . . . faster . . . we are going home . . . the needle will come out . . . needles belong in machines . . . let me blow on your finger . . . open your eyes . . . here! I am breaking the machines! I am smashing them just for you! Here they go one by one! There is nothing left of them! The bell is down . . . no more . . . we are alone. . . .

GITEL

We are not alone . . . something is calling to us . . . let us go [*Like sleepwalkers they step down stage . . . her hands flutter in the air.*] see . . . I am waving to them. . . .

REUBEN

Your hands are like drumsticks beating against the heart of the world. . . .

GITEL

They are frightened . . . they are running away . . . we are after them. . . .

REUBEN

The measures taken by your feet are like thunder rolling over mountain peaks. . . .

GITEL

They are hungry . . . I shall give them my breasts. . . .

REUBEN

I, too, am hungry and your breasts will be like knobs opening new worlds to me. . . .

GITEL

Something has struck them . . . they are falling to earth . . . I remember now . . . I remember. . . .

REUBEN

On your brow are impressed the memories that cling to earth. . . .

GITEL

I am flying . . . come with me . . . come with me . . . I am going high . . . my head is touching sun, moon, stars . . . the wheels are turning too fast . . . the belt caught . . . I am looking for a hiding place. . . .

REUBEN

Your head is a planet searching for a hiding place. . . .

THE MACHINES

Whirrrrr!

GITEL

The belt caught my foot . . . foreman! Foreman! my finger . . . my finger! the needle!
[*Long pause.* REUBEN *holds her closely.*]

GITEL AND REUBEN

[*Tenderly.*] We have found a hiding place. . . .
[LOUIS *comes out from nowhere and glides over to them.*]

LOUIS

Lovin' it up? Youse want a room for fifty cents?
[*The two separate immediately;* REUBEN *walking off and* GITEL *going upstairs.* LOUIS *starts to follow* GITEL *but* ELKE *blocks the the way.*]

ELKE

Go back!

LOUIS

Say what you think you're doing—let me go up!

ELKE

Go back . . . you're not going up!

LOUIS

I'll call Yoshke if you don't let me go!

ELKE

Call all the forces of hell!
[LOUIS *whistles and* YOSHKE *is on the scene.*]

LOUIS

What's got into her head? She won't let me——

ELKE

They are poor people and their life is not too
happy . . . you've ruined enough lives . . . let
them live in peace.

YOSHKE

Pass and let her fall toward me. Go ahead, Louis.
[LOUIS *goes up. To* ELKE.] I'll settle with you tonight.

ELKE

Yoshke, there is a curse to be found in the Talmud, a curse that will be thrown upon you from
behind your back, and it will . . .

YOSHKE

You've cursed me plenty and it ain't done me no
harm yet. I can stand them. *And* my back ain't
never turned. [*Goes into the saloon. . . .* ELKE
walks down the street. LOUIS *knocks on tenement
door.*]

On the Stairs

CHAVE

[*Coming to door.*] What do you want?

LOUIS

Is The Shames in?

CHAVE

No. Do you want The Shames? Are you sure you want The Shames?

LOUIS

Yeah— [*Runs back to saloon.*] Tough luck, Yoshke, her mother was there. Better luck next time.

> [*It is getting dark now . . . night . . . there are a few candles burning in the synagogue . . . Zwi and Chono sit in one corner, prayer books in hand: in another corner is the Rabbi, a large tome before him, holding an argumentative discussion with himself . . . now and then his body becomes electrified . . . his voice lyrical and ecstatic . . . Zwi and Chono mumble too, but their chief occupation is to guard themselves from the Rabbi's forbidding glances.*]

In the Synagogue

ZWI

Mmmmmmmm the Sabbath is the holiest of days
. . . mmmmmmmmm give me a piece of thy bread and
I will give thee some of my dried apples . . . and
watch out for the Rabbi. . . .

CHONO

Yes, the old eagle is watching us. Where didst
thou get the dried apples?

ZWI

From the widow in the cellar store.

CHONO

Making love to that female, art thou?

ZWI

[*Matter-of-fact tone.*] Why not? I still have an
eye for a pretty woman and they do not despise
me. . . . In my youth, I had much love business.

CHONO

Not more than I—I had four wives, do not forget.

ZWI

Four wives you had, and I had three, but what is
a wife to love? I am speaking of love. . . . Ah,

the time I carried a maiden to the river . . . ah, ah. . . .

CHONO

Piffpopoo . . . that is nothing . . . I had love business with a dozen maidens in my time, and more love than you ever dreamed of.

ZWI

You are always jealous of me, and is it not strange, for you know yourself that when I was a student in the great Yeshiva, maidens would come from far away to look at me, and make eyes at me, and bring me dried apples, and cakes and give me locks of their hair . . . that was love . . . Shir Hashirim . . . which is the song of songs.

Let him kiss me with the kisses of his mouth;
For thy love is better than wine.
[CHONO *covers his ears.*]
Thine ointments have a goodly fragrance;
Thy name is as ointment poured forth;
Therefore do the virgins love thee . . .
Therefore do the virgins love the . . . mmmmmmmmm
lalalalammmlala . . . ah, that was love!

CHONO

Piffpoopoo . . . how about the daughter of the innkeeper that would walk in the coldest winter nights to hear me rehearse my lectures? I would have married her, but the Talmud said: one wife is trouble enough.

ZWI

[*In singsong.*] You have no voice now, but my countenance has changed little since my youth, and that is why I still find favor with the females.
Behold, thou art fair, my beloved, yea pleasant:
Also our couch is green.

CHONO

Your love is like your dried apples . . . bahbah . . . piffpoopoo . . .

ZWI

You are an old scropion concerning whom the great Rabbi Akiba said . . .

CHONO

He spoke of you . . . of you . . .

CHONO

Of you . . . you [*They are shouting in each other's faces.*] I'll show you word for word . . . word . . . passion is in my blood . . . the passion of Solomon and you are a— [*The* RABBI *looks at them.*] The Sabbath is the holiest of days. [*They both mumble feverishly.*]

RABBI

[*Looking before him.*] How empty is the house
of the lord . . . like a wind hiding in a crevice
. . . like a bird shorn of its wings . . . like a song
that has lost its melody. . . . Hide, synagogue
. . . hide from shame and degradation for thy glory
is the past . . . Zwi! Chono! Wake up and let
us say the prayers! Asleep! Fakers! The old have
gone to sleep . . . the young trades and despises the
Sabbath. . . . Where to, Israel . . . where to?
What is the goal that thou hast set for thyself,
that thou must leave behind thee thy god and thy
people? Is there no one to hear my voice? Is there
no one to give me answer? This is but a wilderness
and my cry is heard by the passing breeze.

[*Long pause.*]

The roll of names is a long one . . .
The roll of names is not a long one.
There are many names on the roll of Israel . . .
There are few names on the roll of Israel.
The roll of names has no marks on it . . .
The roll of names has many marks on it.
The sky is speckled with stars
They light the earth
One by one the stars fall
And the earth is black.

[ELKE *appears in the doorway.*]

ELKE

Rabbi . . .

[*The* RABBI *jumps up and seeing* ELKE *covers his face with his hands.*]

RABBI

What is it, woman?

ELKE

Rabbi, I have come to . . .

RABBI

What is your name, woman?

ELKE

I do not want to mention it in this holy place.

RABBI

What is your wish?

ELKE

I am a mother and that is my crime. . . . I have a son, this son. . . . I cannot speak any more, Rabbi . . . look into my eyes . . . you can see.

[*The* RABBI *uncovers his face and looks at her fixedly.*]

RABBI

I see pain and tragedy but you must speak more . . . what has this son done to you?

ELKE

I cannot speak any more. . . .

RABBI

Open your heart, woman . . . open your heart,
for I have seen and I have heard of the iniquity of
man.

ELKE

I . . . cannot . . .
[Zwi *and* Chono *are awake now. . . .* Zwi *is
signaling to the* Rabbi. Elke *walks to the
door.* Zwi *runs to the* Rabbi *and whispers
in his ear.*]

RABBI

What . . . what . . . come here, woman . . .
come here . . . call your son here and we shall hold
judgment between you.

ELKE

He will not come.

RABBI

Will not come? I'll send The Shames after him.
If he does not come then, I'll call him myself. Chono,
tell The Shames that I want him to call that son of
hers, and you, Zwi, call a member of the congregation here at once.

ZWI AND CHONO

Yes, Rabbi. [*They leave.*]

[*The* RABBI *becomes animated . . . opens a
huge tome and reads the text before him in
a singsong tone. . . . At the same time we
hear several voices warbling "Alexander's
Ragtime Band."*]

In the Saloon

[*The saloon is in holiday attire:* FLOSSIE *is on*
YOSHKE'S *lap. They finish the song and
there is a round of applause.*]

YOSHKE

Keep it up . . . I'm celebratin' to-night . . . tonight's my night . . . the drinks on me . . . stand
them up . . . tonight's my night.

FLOSSIE

Hey, Louis, got your people all lined up?

LOUIS

Don't need it. Me gat gives orders and they
moves like I tells 'em to.

ALL

Hooray, hooray, hooray!

FLOSSIE

Bet your mother ain't gonna vote for you! Say, you ought to get her a long-term sweetie—she needs someone to keep her warm.

LOUIS

[*Singing.*] She's my Yiddishe love. . . . Be kind to all the ladies, says the constitution!

YOSHKE

I'd marry her off to the Polack in the basement; he's lonely, the poor bastard. . . .

LOUIS

Sometimes she goes down there so soft I can't hear her steps.

FLOSSIE

You'd better take a drink . . . pretty soon you'll have to make your appearance before the lousy august people.
    [THE SHAMES *enters humbly and whispers in* YOSHKE'S *ear.*]

YOSHKE

WHAT? [*Throws* THE SHAMES *aside.*]

FLOSSIE

What's the matter?

YOSHKE

Shut up, Flossie, this is my business! Who sent you?

THE SHAMES

The Rabbi.

YOSHKE

Who in the hell is he? What right he got to call me? You ain't bluffing me on this, are you?

FLOSSIE

You'd better do it, Yoshke. You got to play the long whiskers . . . got to!

YOSHKE

All right . . . all right . . . but I'll break my mother's face for this. Hold 'em off a while, Shames, let 'em wait. I've got to fix something up. I'll straighten it out with you. [*To* FLOSSIE.] Free drinks and cigars for any lousy chisling bum that looks like he's got a vote.

FLOSSIE

Hell, that ain't hard, I can fix that easy.

YOSHKE

Come on, Louis, let's scare up the parade.

LOUIS

Wait'll I gets my gats. [*He and* THE SHAMES *walk out. An alarm clock rings furiously.*]

In the Tenement

GITEL

Mother! Mother! Stop that clock! Stop it! Mother, I am not going back to that shop . . . I am afraid to work there. . . . Every time I go in that place, my heart . . . we are being crushed and torn there . . . something is going to happen there one of these days . . . I feel it . . . here . . . feel my heart . . . it is not mine . . . not mine . . . a sewing machine is there . . . don't you hear it? It is changing stitches now . . . shorter longer . . . why must we stay here: are there no other places in the world?

CHAVE

We cannot go everywhere . . . we must stay here . . . very few doors are open to us . . . here there is opportunity.

GITEL

Opportunity? Does it mean planting a rose in a dungheap? Cutting your throat to quench your thirst?

CHAVE

My child, this is the first time in my life I am not afraid to open my eyes.

GITEL

How can we see with the smoke and the dust in our eyes?

CHAVE

We shall soon have something to be thankful for: father . . . is . . . making a . . . living . . . he is. . . .

GITEL

Father making a living?   God's valet always ate from someone else's plate.

CHAVE

But he is doing something now . . . something came into his hands today. . . . Yankel is making money and is studious . . . he'll be a lawyer soon. . . . He is coming home.

[YANKEL *rushes in.*]

YANKEL

Hello!   Anything to eat?   Got to go to school. . . . Made two fifteen today and I found . . .

CHAVE

Hush!   Keep your finding to yourself.   What are you selling now?

YANKEL

Yesterday I sold silk shawls.   Today, picture postcards from Paris, 2 for 25.   Wanna see them, sister?   Say, what's she bawling about?   Will she ever be satisfied?   Ain't she got a job?   A home?

Didn't she want to come here? Why don't you be like me? I work in the day and go to school at night time. . . . I belong to three clubs. I ain't got no time to bawl. I'm goin' to be a lawyer and then an inspector like Yoshke and run for alderman and be a leader. Say, what time is it? Gee, I'm late. Guess I'll eat when I come back. I'm goin' to be a judge, too, some day. So long . . . save supper for me. [*Runs out.*]

CHAVE

Did you see that? Did you see the spirit that's in him?

GITEL

Is that the spirit that drives the machines and men . . . ? Give me your breast, mother . . . perhaps I may still find some of that spirit left to nourish me . . . then I'll marry a machine and have little machines and their fingers will be needles . . . the heads will be wheels and the feet walking beams. . . . [*Sleepily.*] If the alarm clock dies . . . wake me up and we'll go to his funeral. . . .

CHAVE

[*To herself.*] At your age, my daughter, I was satisfied with the world. . . . I had no dreams such as you have, for my tresses and my life were laid out for me . . . when you were within me, I had dreams for you . . . let no one judge between us, for my dreams were for you, and I had no thoughts from which you were barred . . . you are judging me, my child—over us a mother is asking judgment against her son. The world of mothers is being judged.

ELKE'S VOICE

[*From the synagogue.*] Let the Rabbi and you holy people judge between us then. . . .

CHAVE

[*Continuing to* GITEL.] Would I bring you into the world to make you the twin of a machine?

ELKE'S VOICE

[*From synagogue.*] Would a mother bring a child into the world to tear him limb from limb? Where, then, is the blood that the loss to one is the loss to the other? The pain of one is the pain of both . . . judge between us then. . . .

CHAVE

[*As above.*] My child, it is your mother Chave speaking to you. Do not let your dreams carry you away from me . . . the stray bird is the prey of the eagle and the body is soft. . . . [*Takes* GITEL *in her arms . . . we begin to discern the synagogue*

scene: the RABBI, THE SHAMES *and the* OLD IMMI-
GRANT *are sitting down;* ELKE *and* YOSHKE *stand
before them.*]

In the Synagogue

ELKE

I did not let him stray from me, for what mother
would not keep her child near her body to nestle and
to nurse?

THE SHAMES

Why, then, did he run around eating at other people's tables?

ELKE

A mother has but two eyes and the world is wide
and long.

THE SHAMES

That is no excuse: a mother's shadow should rest
over her children.

RABBI

These things were wrong of the mother: what
wrongs did the son commit after the age of thirteen?

YOSHKE

They would not let me in the synagogue and so I
never became of age according to the law.

RABBI

So you have never had phelacteries on your head and arm?

YOSHKE

I never did.

RABBI

[*To* ELKE.] Did not his father know that he was breaking a law of Israel by denying him entrance to the synagogue?

YOSHKE

He had too much pride in him.

ELKE

When a man has a growth upon his body does he not cut it off? But my son would not change his evil ways.

YOSHKE

That is it! That's always been their answer! Look what parents' pride gave me! [*Throws off his coat and shows his bare chest and back marked and scarred.*]

THE SHAMES

Look at that! Was there no mercy in your hearts?

YOSHKE

They had mercy for the horse!

OLD IMMIGRANT

In the old world the children obeyed their parents, but it is not so in this land: this is a new land.

RABBI

The code of law is the same.

OLD IMMIGRANT

But the fathers and sons are not the same: there you gave him bread and bed: here he gives you bread and bed.

RABBI

Israel does not change, nor do her laws change: "Honor thy father and thy mother." [THE SHAMES *whispers to the* RABBI.] What is the opinion of a servant to me! We are not judging in favor of one because he is strong and against another because he is weak. [*To* YOSHKE.] You understand that?

YOSHKE

I do. I didn't have to come here . . . you couldn't force me to, but I wanted to be heard so that my own people would know that I am not as bad as I am painted. I am still a son of my people.

RABBI

If you are still a son of your people, why then do you live by force and make shame and evil your profession?

YOSHKE

That is my business, not yours.

ELKE

There you have the spirit of my son.

OLD IMMIGRANT

In this land the parents should obey their sons:
Woman, what is left thee but to obey?

ELKE

That's why I came here . . . here . . . to
you. . . .

OLD IMMIGRANT

Does he now give you bread and a bed to sleep in?

ELKE

But the bread is bitter and I cannot close my
eyes.

THE SHAMES

I say that the son is right.

OLD IMMIGRANT

In this land the son is before the father: I waited
many weeks before my son came to see me, although
he brought me here, for I said that this is a new land,
and master is he who has the key to the lock.

RABBI

But that is not the way of the Talmud, and I shall not pass judgment in favor of the son.

YOSHKE

Two holy men have judged in my favor and I do not need your word.

RABBI

You cannot go away from here until I have released you from your bond: for did you not swear that you would abide by my word?

YOSHKE

I have broken as many words as they have broken sticks over me. That is nothing new to me. . . . [*Looks out.*] There is a parade soon to start to do me honor!

THE SHAMES

[*To* RABBI.] They do him honor . . . he is to be an alderman soon . . . that is a high honor— and would they honor a man who has been harsh to his mother?

OLD IMMIGRANT

The young hold life and death in their hands and honor is due them because they have captured the new world.

RABBI

But I shall not honor him. . . .

YOSHKE

This is a poor place for a synagogue: I do not want my own people to be my enemies: I will donate——

RABBI

I shall not honor you for all the money in the world! But I shall curse you to the end of eternity!

ELKE

[*Standing up, pleads with the* RABBI.] He has been cursed enough, Rabbi! Let it be! I'll atone for him!

RABBI

[*Bitterly.*] Female, thou art no better than thy son! I wash my hands of the both of you!

> [*On the street a crowd has formed . . . sounds of tins horns, ratchets, whistles; placards reading: "Joseph Shafer, Candidate for Alderman: An Honest and Capable Man" . . . "Vote for the People's Favorite" . . . "Joseph Shafer, Regular Party Candidate for Alderman." . . .* LOUIS *is shoving the people about, threatening, cajoling and forcing them on.*]

YOSHKE

[*On stairs.*] Come on, come on! [*Parade comes on from the left.*] Come on, come on.

LOUIS

March, march, march on!

YOSHKE

Hey, youse, I got it all fixed up with the Rabbi. We are friends from now on. Me and him patched it all up.

LOUIS AND MOB

Hooray!

YOSHKE

I tell you, you got to vote for me now, because if you don't, you'll be the losers. Get me? I keep promises and if you don't believe it, ask the guys what knows it. The peddlers'll give you an earful. I'm being backed solid by everybody that's got a vote and as Joseph Shafer, standing before you now, figures it: everybody that wants to vote for me has a vote.

LOUIS AND MOB

Hooray! Hooray!

YOSHKE

To the hall, the hall, the hall!

[*Signaling to* LOUIS, *he heads the parade, which*

moves off shouting, singing, . . . Louis *is
seen everywhere . . . his right hand in his
pocket, jostling people . . . kicking them,
urging them on.*]

LOUIS

March, march, march on! [*He shoves* Zwi, *who
stands gaping at the procession, with such force
that the other falls down.*]

ZWI

What you pushin' for—he pushes, what you
pushin'? He pushes!

LOUIS

It's for Yoshke Shtarker!

ZWI

Ai, ai, ai, for Yoshke Shtarker! Ai, ai, ai.
[*Takes out a tin cup and shakes it.*] For Yoshke
Shtarker—have mercy on his soul! Charity
will. . . .

LOUIS

Shut up, he ain't dead: he's runnin' for alderman!

ZWI

What! That crook, that grafter running for
——? [Louis *knocks him down.*]

LOUIS

Say another word and I'll nail you!

ZWI

Let him run for president, he's strong enough!
Hooray! Hooray! Hooray!
[*Marches off in front of* LOUIS.]

CHONO

Police, Police!
[LOUIS *turns and threatens him.*]
Hooray, hooray!
[*They join the paraders. The stage is clear.*
VLADISLAV *is standing in front of his base-
ment.*]

VLADISLAV

That noise, what does it mean? They wake me
up. [*Looks about, but seeing no one, speaks to
himself.*] Nobody to ask, go back to sleep, maybe
it's a party . . . some day I'll give a party . . .
who's going to come? Got no one . . . no use
giving party, no use . . . go back to sleep. [ELKE
is coming down the street.] There comes that
woman . . . she's lonely, too, but she's got lots of
men and women . . . she shouldn't be lonely . . .
maybe she'll have some tea. . . . I'll make some tea
for her and me . . . maybe she'll talk to me. . . .
Hello!

ELKE

Hello! [*Stops and waits.*]

VLADISLAV

I . . . I . . . am sleepy . . . I go . . . to sleep, tomorrow lots of work . . . good night. . . . [*Goes down.*]

ELKE

Good night! [*She goes up.*]
[*The noise of the parade is still heard when the curtains close.*]

THIRD ACT

Farewell to ourselves——We die for your shirt
——Tabernacle of the Penny Jehovah——Litany of
the mother superior——Step down Moses——

* * * * * * *

[*Early morning. The curtains part . . . there*
has been one change on the street: the candy store
has blossomed forth into a pawn shop. There is a
light there and we hear voices. The workers are
going to the factory.]

THE MACHINES

Whirrrr . . . whirrrrrr . . . whirrrrrrrrr

On the Street

[VLADISLAV *is just going out to work. . . .*
GITEL *emerges from the pawn shop and stands*
there waiting. The couple appears and the
YOUNG MAN *knocks on the door of the shop.*]

YOUNG MAN

Mister! Mister! We want a letter written by
you to the old country. [*Pause.*] Wake up, do you
hear me? We want a letter written to the old country—it's an important letter and we'll pay for the
paper and there'll be no argument.

126

THE SHAMES' VOICE

Gerarehere—I don't write letters any more—
gerarehere!

YOUNG WOMAN

But who's going to write a letter for us if you
don't? You've been writing them all the time—
Mister!

YOUNG MAN

Mister, do you hear me?

LOUIS

[*Pushing his head through the open door.*] Get
the hell away from here, before I knock your blocks
off! [*Goes in.*]

YOUNG MAN

What did I do? I didn't do. [*Gesticulates.*]

GITEL

Where do you work?

YOUNG WOMAN

Mind your own business!

GITEL

I think we work in the same place.

YOUNG WOMAN

Maybe—there's lots of people working there—
lots.

GITEL

If that letter is important, I'll write it for you during the lunch hour.

YOUNG MAN

How can you write? A girl can write? Did you hear that, Faige? A girl can write!

YOUNG WOMAN

I don't believe it. How can you write when you work like we do? You think I am a cow that I don't understand anything? You ought to see how much money I make in that shop. The foreman says I'm the best stitcher he's got. Then she tries to make a cow out of me. You can't do it, I'm telling you. It's not for nothing that I work in the shop where I learn a lot of things about the world.

GITEL

[*With a sigh.*] Just the same, if my father won't write the letter for you, I will.

YOUNG MAN

Did you hear that, Faige? Her father is the one that used to write the letters for us.

YOUNG WOMAN

Nu that's different . . . so . . . excuse me . . . but you won't take any money for it?

GITEL

I'll do it as favor.

YOUNG MAN

Good-by!

YOUNG WOMAN

Good-by and excuse me. . . .

YOUNG MAN

[*To* GITEL *as he and the* YOUNG WOMAN *walk off.*] You'll be late.

GITEL

I hope so.
    [*A young working girl comes out of a flat, followed by an elderly woman—her mother.*]

THE MOTHER

Don't lose the lunch . . . don't lose it . . . you hear me? Don't eat it too fast, it's bad for you . . . [*Follows the girl.*] . . . and don't be afraid: noise can't hurt you . . . wipe your eyes every half hour; I put a clean handkerchief with the lunch: the dust won't get in your eyes then—and look out of the window: when you see the sky you won't be afraid.

THE DAUGHTER

There are no windows near me.

GITEL

There is no sky!

THE MOTHER

The lord will protect you . . . good-by . . .
good-by . . . I'll wait for you for supper. I'll
wait for you . . . sit near the window . . . near the
window . . . near the window, do you hear me?
[*But the girl is away off . . . she runs after her.*]
Look at the sky . . . wipe your eyes: I'll wait for
you. . . .

[GITEL *sees* REUBEN *and walks toward him.*]

REUBEN

Hello!

GITEL

I thought you'd never come . . . you missed
something here . . . that mother said farewell to
her daughter . . . it seemed as if this girl was going away, far away—perhaps forever . . . then
that couple that always walks by itself . . . the
couple that looks as if its ancestors were farm
animals . . . that is always chewing things . . .
wanted a letter written, but father is too busy dis-
cussing law with a pimp and a gangster . . . they
were so pitiful . . . they don't belong in a shop. . . .

REUBEN

What are we waiting for?

GITEL

Hoping we'll be late . . . they say they've got
many orders now . . . they are hiring more cutters
and operators . . . two shifts . . . yesterday my
elbow was stopped all the time by Lena's face, she
was so close to me; her face was red and blotchy
when the gong rang. I told my mother last night
that one of these days we'd go on strike. My
brother said it was against the law to talk that way.
My brother is a lawyer.

REUBEN

Life is against the law.

GITEL

Reuben, let's go to school instead.

REUBEN

To school?

GITEL

Yes. We're not too old, are we?

REUBEN

But what will the foreman say?

GITEL

But what will the teacher say?

REUBEN

Come on!

GITEL

Stop! Count to a hundred before we move again!

REUBEN

Why?

GITEL

Forty, forty-one, forty-two,—so that we'll have an excuse to be late.

REUBEN

Come on! The Avenue needs silk waists!

GITEL

The Avenue needs silk shrouds . . . [*They are walking off slowly*] fourteen . . . thirteen . . . twelve. . . .

REUBEN

You're cheating . . . [*They do a ring around the rosie.*]

GITEL

Let's start all over again!
[*They go.*]

[THE VEGETABLE PEDDLER *comes on quickly and furtively.*]

THE VEGETABLE PEDDLER

Vegetables! Hurry up! Vegetables! [*The* MOTHER *rushes down and begins picking out vegetables.*] HURRY up, hurry up, Missus!

THE MOTHER

What's the hurry? He's in a hurry!

THE VEGETABLE PEDDLER

The inspector, the inspector!

THE MOTHER

Nu, what about the inspector?

THE VEGETABLE PEDDLER

He said no peddlers on this street. . . . Have no license, hurry up! Nu, nu, nu . . .

THE MOTHER

All the curses in the Talmud on the inspector and you . . . the vegetables are for my daughter . . . she works in a big shop where they make——

THE VEGETABLE PEDDLER

Hurry up, hurry up, hurry up!

THE MOTHER

She supports me and I keep the house and I cook
. . . so I've got to choose the vegetables and if the
inspector doesn't like it he can dance on one foot
. . . nu, nu, how much?—they're rotten, anyway. . . .

THE VEGETABLE PEDDLER

They're not rotten, because you didn't pick rotten ones,—eighteen cents.

THE MOTHER

I can't afford that: ten cents!

THE VEGETABLE PEDDLER

You piece of rotten radish, you want to get me
in trouble keeping me so long,—sixteen cents: give
me the money.

THE MOTHER

You think my daughter makes gold . . . she
makes shirtwaists: twelve cents!

THE VEGETABLE PEDDLER

I hope you never see your daughter, you . . .
you . . .

[*The vegetables fall out of* THE MOTHER's
hands . . . there is a movement in the saloon

. . . The Peddler *rushes off* . . . The Mother *stands glued to the ground.* Elke *comes out and, seeing the old woman, goes over to her . . . the latter screams and rushes upstairs. . . .* Elke *goes back to the saloon entrance.*]

THE MACHINES

Whirrrr . . . whirrrrrr . . . whirrrrrrrrrrrr . . .
[The Mother *comes down again hurriedly, a shawl thrown over her shoulders . . . looks around and seeing no one sidles over to* Elke, *but does not look at her.*]

THE MOTHER

I want to go to the shop . . . to the shop. . . .

ELKE

What shop?

THE MOTHER

To the shop . . . to the shop where my daughter works. . . .

ELKE

Which shop is it? On what street?

THE MOTHER

How do I know? What do I know of a shop? How do I come to a shop? My daughter works there, that's all I know . . . where is it?

ELKE

I don't know.

THE MOTHER

You're a woman of the world and I only go to the synagogue or stay at home . . . you ought to know where the shop is . . . where is it?

ELKE

I don't know where that shop is . . . has it no name?

THE MOTHER

You sinful woman, you know where that shop is and you won't tell a mother where her daughter is . . . oh . . . oh . . . !

ELKE

Why shouldn't I want to tell you where your child is? Haven't I had children of my own? But I don't know where this shop is.

THE MOTHER

[*Walking away.*] You know where she is . . . you know . . . where is my child . . . oh, where is my child . . . something has happened to my child and they won't tell me where she is. . . .

ELKE

How do you know that anything has happened to your child?

THE MOTHER

There is the gift of prophecy in every mother . . . it is given to her when her first born looks into her eyes. . . . [*She walks up to the head of the stairs and remains there . . . pleading to the world.*]

ELKE

All the evil in the world is blamed upon me . . . I am a wolf . . . a snake . . . a lion . . . daughters and wives . . . I am their keeper. . . .

In the Factory

[THE OFFICE GIRL *is at the telephone,* THE BOSS *at her side . . . they seem to be swimming in the air.*]

THE GIRL

[*Frantically.*] Fire Department! Fire Department! Fire Department!

THE BOSS

Fire Department Z and W Shop—tell them Z and W Shop.

THE GIRL

Z and W Shop Z and W Shop Fire Department Fire Department!

THE BOSS

Police Department Police Department Fire Department Police Police Fire!

THE GIRL

Police Z and W Shop Emergency Emergency Fire Z and W Shop!

THE BOSS

Call the ambulance the ambulance the police the Fire Department!

THE BOSS AND THE GIRL

Fire Department, Police, Ambulance Z and W, Z and W Shop, Shop Emergency, Emergency, Accident Fire Hurry . . . Hurry. . . .

[THE BOSS *dashes off* . . . THE GIRL *sinks to the ground.* . . . THE MACHINES *stop abruptly with a crash* . . . *second crash* . . . *third crash* . . . *sky is streaked with red ribbons.* . . . ELKE *falls to the ground.* . . . THE MOTHER's *hands go out before her, as if reaching for someone* . . . *her mouth opens, but no sound is heard* . . . *she tries*

*to walk, but all she can do is move her torso
forward and then fall back . . . finally she
cries out . . . a house bell rings violently
. . . a woman rushes out madly and off towards right . . . a policeman dashes on
. . . fierce blasts on police whistles . . .
there is a kind of humming noise in the air
. . . a murmur of a thousand winds . . .
the stage is growing dark . . . measured
beats on kettle drums tell of off the beating
of a huge heart . . . MOVEMENT . . . cries
. . . movement. . . . Chaos . . . men and
women are rushing madly here and there
. . . fire, police ambulance bells ring wildly
in unison and singly . . . the stage is com-
pletely dark . . . cries . . . movement and
then an awful silence broken finally by the
sounds of coins rattling in tin cups and the
voices of old men and women chanting. . . .]*

On the Street

VOICES

Charity will save you from death . . . charity
will save you from death . . . Chdoko tachil mmoves
. . . chdoko tachil mmoves . . . charity will save
you from death . . . charity will save you from
death . . . chdoko tachil mmoves. . . .

[We hear and feel a mass in motion . . .]

CHAVE'S VOICE

My daughter! Have you seen my daughter, Gitel—she worked in that shop! Have you seen my daughter?

VOICES

Charity will save you from death . . . chdoko tachil mmoves. . . .

OTHER VOICES

Hospital . . . doctor . . . ambulance . . . where? *Where? . . . Hospital.* . . .

VOICES

Charity will save you from death . . . chdoko tachil mmoves . . . chdoko tachil mmoves. . . .

[*A single light picks out* REUBEN *on the stairway.*]

A VOICE OFFSTAGE

Here are the names!

REUBEN

Victims of the Z and W shop fire identified!

VOICE, THEN REUBEN

Rose Golstein, Lena Bressler, Santi Giovanni, Esther Cohen, Reba Wetowitz, Joseph Hoffman, Hyman Chetlow, Isidor Feitelbaum, Leah Otnitz. . . .

REUBEN

These are all the names we have now. . . .
[THE MOTHER *is sitting on the ground, several
women with her.*]

THE MOTHER

When you nurse a child you nurse his tears and
his joys . . . his birth and his death . . . you give
him ten things to remember, ten to forget . . . for
the mother goes into the child, and the child takes
the world of the mother, and the mother goes into
the earth, but woe to the mother, when the child
goes into the earth first . . . oh, what a country, to
take the child before its mother . . . what a country, to go against the ways of the lord . . . what
a burden the rest of my days are going to be upon
me . . . shma Yisrael hear my voice . . . let my
breath die on my lips for the name of my child has
been erased. . . .
[*The Mass is moving on.*]

VOICES

Charity will save you from death . . . chdoko
tachil mmoves. . . .

REUBEN

Ruth Garfinkle, Rose Mayer, Portnoy—first name
not known. . . .

[*At the synagogue the funeral service is being
conducted by the* RABBI *and a group of old
men.*]

In the Synagogue

VOICES

Chdoko tachil mmoves . . . charity will save you
from death. . . .

RABBI

El mole rachmin shonrim. . . .

MOURNERS

Ishkadak v'ishkadash shmai rabbo. . . .
[*The Mass is still moving . . . the humming is
still heard . . . the prayers are a murmur
now. . . .*]

VOICES

Charity will save you from death . . . chdoko
tachil mmoves. . . .

REUBEN

Charity will not save you from death!

VOICES

Charity will save you from death . . . chdoko
tachil mmoves. . . .

REUBEN

Farewell to ourselves! There is life . . . death
. . . charity . . . there is no life or charity for

you, but there is death . . . move on and bury your
dead . . . let us speak in this hour of grief for those
whose tongues are silent and act for those who are
beyond action.

GITEL

Farewell to ourselves! This morning there was a
mother saying good-by to her daughter . . . the
mother knew: the daughter knew . . . she has just
been identified, but there are thousands to take her
place . . . there are enough machines, enough shirtwaists, enough fire for them all. . . .

REUBEN AND GITEL

Farewell to ourselves!

REUBEN

In remembering those who have gone, let us not
forget those who are to come . . . what remains
for us? What is there left for us to do?

A VOICE NEAR THE FACTORY

Here are two more names: Faige and her friend,
Max Spivack!

REUBEN

Two more names: Faige and her friend, Max
Spikack!

GITEL

This morning I wrote a letter for them to their old people at home . . . they told them of their happiness . . . of their love for each other, of the fine home they were fixing up and promised to enclose pictures with the next letter. Call the photographers and let's send the proud old parents a picture to remember Columbus's land!!

VOICES

Charity will save you from death . . . chdoko tachil mmoves. . . .

REUBEN

Now that we have buried our dead are we ready to go back and receive our share? Arise, you workers of starvation!

GITEL

Arise, you prisoners of the earth!

VOICES

Charity will save you from death . . . chdoko tachil mmoves. . . .

GITEL

Men and women of the sweat shops! What need is there of home, of labor, of wages, if there is no

life! Let us not go back to the shops until we
know that our lives are safe! No fire traps! No
sweat shops! Let us stop the machines that pound
life out of us!

RABBI

Strike? You cannot strike! That must not be
the answer! These dead were being punished for
their sins!

REUBEN

The voice of god! Our dead brothers and sisters
were punished for their sins! It was a sin to work
in a sweatshop! It was a sin to die for a shirtwaist!
It was a sin to live at all!

RABBI

I warn you that catastrophe will descend upon
you if you strike! It is against the law of the
country and of the lord! You must work! Work!
Work! For your wives and your children and your
old parents depend upon you! Heed my words!
You are young! Heed the words of an old and
wise man! In Russia they slaughtered young and
old because they dared to go against the law! I
stood up in the synagogue and advised them to obey
the law, but they shouted me down and then they
went to their deaths! The law of the land is the
law of God!

GITEL

Yes, that is the Rabbi who had chained revolutionists brought to him to the synagogue that he may point to them as a warning to other workers! That is the man who prayed that these prisoners be punished with death! That is the lackey of the murderers! He brought his venom, his voice of doom along with his prayers! He is crying now because he cannot have us chained and brought to him to sit in judgment of us! If we are to be doomed, let him be doomed, too!

REUBEN

While we are burying our comrades let us also bury this refuse left in the old house, let us bury this ornament of the ghetto! Is it our will that the machines stop?

FIRST VOICE

Strike! [*Raises fist in air.*]

SECOND VOICE

Strike! [*Raises fist.*]

CHORUS OF VOICES

Strike! [*Fists in the air.*]

REUBEN

Let the machines stop!
 [*Whistles are blown.*]

GITEL

The strike is declared! Strike! Strike! Strike!

REUBEN

Keep order! Move in pairs! Order! Order!
Order! Move in pairs!
 [*The Mass divides itself and marches double file
 back and forth. Police patrol gong . . .
 the pickets keep on moving. A flat: Wife is
 setting table. Striker comes in.*]

In a Flat

STRIKER

Strike is declared. . . . [WIFE *looks at him un-
believingly.*] It is going to be a long strike. . . .
[WIFE *removes a few plates.*] Why are you taking
the food away?

WIFE

Save it . . . going to be a long strike . . . we'll
need it later . . .
 [*The march of the pickets becomes faster. . . .*]

THE CURTAINS CLOSE

FOURTH ACT

In the Saloon

[*The saloon:* YOSHKE *and* LOUIS.]

YOSHKE

Louis, this strike's workin' out all right—it's goin' to be big pickin': a lot of janes out of work —no home an' no board soon: good chance, an' I told my mother to take care of that, an' she'd better do it, too . . . I got a big job cleanin' the streets in front of the shops . . . ten shops an' I got to keep fixin' the cops too, so they don' get too warm with the strikers. . . .

LOUIS

I don' get this straight,—which side are you on?

YOSHKE

Jesus, you're dumb—the bosses. . . . I got to keep the strikers away from the shops, see that they don' get inside, an' if they keep on winnin', butcher or plug 'em.

LOUIS

[*Stalling.*]   You mean you're on the side of the guys that owns the shops?   [*Backs away.*]

YOSHKE

Yes, whadja think . . . whatsa matter?

LOUIS

Nothin', just wanted to know.

YOSHKE

Now what the hell are youse drivin' at?   Come out with it, Louis, or I'll get mad as hell.

LOUIS

I just thought I'd go out an' get a little work for myself, that's all.

YOSHKE

What kind of work?

LOUIS

Maybe a job keepin' the sluggers off'n the strikers.   [*Long pause.*]

YOSHKE

Well, that's all right . . . guess it is . . . I don't care which side youse is on as long as you works wid me.

LOUIS

But if I work on the other side how can I work wid you?

YOSHKE

All I got to say is don't touch my men, or I'll plug you stiff.

LOUIS

Not so fast, Yoshke, what the hell is wrong wid you . . . can't I ever grow up an' work on my own hook? Jesus, here I worked a good job for the Shames an' the old bastard give me enough to buy worm soup, an' all because you gets a rake off an' . . .

YOSHKE

Say, don' I have to pay his son somethin' for keepin' mum . . . ? All he got to do is open his lip an' youse is a goner for sure.

LOUIS

He ain't goin' to pass you up, is he?

YOSHKE

He can't squeal on me because we're members of the same party an' the boss wouldn't stan' for it, an' he knows how fast I can work if I get mad. . . . Jesus, here he comes. . . . [*Throws a deck of cards on the table and they feign playing.* YANKEL *enters.*]

YANKEL

Say, how do you boys stand on this strike?

YOSHKE

What strike are youse talkin' about?

YANKEL

Oh, come on, the garment strike!

YOSHKE

Keepin' clear of it.

YANKEL

Sure? There's been a dozen jobs done already by some gang . . . ain't yours, is it?

YOSHKE

Nothin' doin'—not me. . . .

YANKEL

I got money here if you guys keep out of this.

YOSHKE

Whose money?

YANKEL

Mine now.

YOSHKE

What's the dope, come out with it!

YANKEL

Want to have the field clear and no butcherin's goin' to be done. Is that on? . . . Your gang's got to stay home.

YOSHKE

What do we get for it?

YANKEL

All depends on the contributions . . . get me? Is that on?

YOSHKE

[*Getting up and facing* YANKEL.] Want me to trust you?

YANKEL

Don't care if you don't, Yoshke, but the captain said so . . . take it or leave it. . . .

YOSHKE

Captain? What gang do you belong to? Ain't the cops, is it?

YANKEL

Maybe. . . . What you got to understand, Yoshke, is this: this town's changing. You're a

back number, get me? Things is run differently
now . . . there's a lot of papers that is out to get
our party because of guys like you. And them
sokalists is hammering away at us. We got to make
a clean job of this . . . there's plenty of money, but
it's got to be pulled out of their pockets in a different way . . . the old stuff don't work no more.

YOSHKE

Say, who in the hell are youse to tell me all them
things? Hey? Before you was spittin' in my spi-
toons I was boss of this section. Who are youse
. . . you . . .

YANKEL

Well, I'm the guy that's standing before you
now, with no gat in my pocket, waitin' for you to
plug me. But you ain't going to do it, because
you're afraid of your own skin. I grew up right
under your nose and I learned everything from
watching you, and a couple of things from the
books, and I'm the guy that's going to tell you
when to clear out of here. That's me. What's
more, I got the boss behind me and the whole damn
machine too, because I belong here . . . them's
the times . . . if you know what I mean. . . . You
never got elected alderman, did you? Well, they
don't want you any more. You're as welcome here
as hellroom in August.

YOSHKE

You're trying to push me out of here, Yank, an'
you got the big mucks behind you, because you're
a lawyer and can read and write maybe. . . . [*Sits
down.*] Go ahead, the gang'll stay home . . . but
we ain't goin' to do it for nothin' . . . we're on,
Yankel—when's pay day?

YANKEL

Collections start today. Call off your men . . .
we got them spotted anyway. . . .

YOSHKE

I'll call them off . . . god dam' sorry, Yankel,
I didn't plug you when you was grabbin' things for
me a couple of years ago . . . you growed up too
fast . . . doin' me plenty you are, but you can read
an' write an' talk to the big mucks an' they're
ashamed of me . . . don' back out of that door
. . . you're safe. . . .

YANKEL

So long. . . . [*Goes out.*]

YOSHKE

Cops is grabbin' our meat . . . this is the first
big strike an' we're goin' to lose out. . . .

LOUIS

Say, Yoshke, maybe this shyster is tryin' to double cross us?

YOSHKE

That ain't nothin' . . . I can always double cross him four times before he turns around . . . say, Louis, I got an idea . . . I works for the shops . . . youse for the union . . . we gets a share from the shyster . . . we cleans up, that's all. . . .

LOUIS

How about the cops?

YOSHKE

Bribe the cops.

LOUIS

Jesus, I'd like to know which side I'm on.

YOSHKE

What the hell difference does it make?

In a Flat

[*A flat: shop girl on chair . . . a single white light.*]

GIRL STRIKER

[*Simply.*] So this is a strike! I ran away from a land that would give you no bread, peace or life. . . . I came here and find work: it brings me bread and life: thin bread and thinner life, but one can always look away off and dream: then they try to take life away: there's plenty of it and they do not care: we refuse to work unless they give us a little air, a bit of sun, and an open door through which we may walk out when our life is threatened: for that, my head is beaten against a wall by a gangster, my back falls on a sidewalk . . . my body goes to pieces. I am here . . . where will my feet carry me from here? I have no home . . . there is no bed waiting for me . . . nor is the table set. . . . So this is a strike!

In the Saloon

YOSHKE

Sure, it don' make no difference which side youse is on, but youse got to try to get handfuls from both sides, because they don' love youse, an' youse don' love them . . . just keep your own skin safe . . . and the lead pipe handy.

In the Flat

GIRL STRIKER

There were many of us, but he picked me out . . . his hands were large . . . he picked me out, but we are all one, for if he had beaten another girl, the bruises would have been on my body too, for we are all one. . . . I looked into his face, scarred and torn like an old sieve left out in the rain. . . . I wanted to ask him "why?" but he was running away, as if I could harm him. . . .

In the Saloon

YOSHKE

Sure youse is safe . . . the guys that gets it in the neck never pay . . . they never know where youse come from or why youse hit them. . . . Hey, Louis, no use keepin' the greenbacks waitin' . . . let's get on the job. [*Picks up lead pipe.*] This baby's waitin' for its mamma.

> [LOUIS *exits up stairway to factory.* YOSHKE *starts up stairs, sees girl through door and goes back to saloon.*]

GIRL STRIKER

I'll go out and take whatever comes . . . I got to live somehow. . . . I might as well forget many things that I learned in the past . . . must look for life where life is to be found. [*Comes down and walks to the pawnshop . . .* THE SHAMES *is at the counter . . . the* GIRL STRIKER *gives him a ring.* YOSHKE *calls* ELKE *and points out the girl to her.*]

In the Pawnshop

THE SHAMES

That's no good—what do I want it for?

GIRL STRIKER

But I need the money.

THE SHAMES

Aha, if my heart was made of gold and I had to give a piece of it to everybody that needed money, what kind of a heart would I have left? There are other ways of making money than by pawning rings.

GIRL STRIKER

What are the ways?

THE SHAMES

This is not a school—go out and learn for yourself . . .

[GIRL *goes out.* ELKE *is standing near the saloon and is eyeing the girl.*]

On the Street

ELKE

Tired? Come in and rest . . . there's no harm . . . don't be afraid . . . lots of girls are out of work . . . lots of them . . . the strike will be a long one and there are a lot of gangsters who have no mercy . . . why be beaten up for nothing? You are too young to be without a home . . . come in and rest . . . I too had no home, but I put everything aside—even my god—for a home . . . a human being needs a home . . . are you coming in? No? Come back some other time . . . yes? When you are very hungry and tired . . . then come

... yes? I understand you like a mother would
... just like a mother ... remember me. ...
[GIRL STRIKER *walks off.*]

In the Pawnshop

THE SHAMES

Business with rings ... with girls ... she needs
money ... is that my business?

CHAVE'S VOICE

[*From behind the counter.*] Since you became
Yoshke's partner you've lost all human feeling ...
ah, ah ... is she not a child? Are you not thankful that your child is safe? What does it matter
if the ring is worth nothing? Since when has a factory girl got to have diamond rings?

THE SHAMES

I am not God and I'm not Rothschild.

CHAVE

A regular allrightnick you've become ... a Jew
among Jews you used to be, lazy but good-natured,
and you used to collect money for the poor, even
though you put half in your pocket for your trouble
and now you've become a ... a pawnshop keeper
... a fence ... ai, ai, ai.

THE SHAMES

Here are some rags, stuff them down your throat,
you dried up fish, you . . . you kept on nagging
me to do something . . . nu, nu, I did. In Europe
I was the slave to every rich man who came into
the synagogue . . . here I am master.

CHAVE

And now Louis steals and Yoshke robs and your
learned son protects you all . . . you did not have
to move your fingers or your lips, and now you're a
wealthy man and a landlord of a synagogue . . .
a partner with the lord, and Louis, and Yoshke
. . . a great country America. . . .

THE SHAMES

In Europe I had to wipe the Rabbi's boots, here I
forbid him to speak to me; there I had to wash the
floors of the synagogue: here I own it. But still
you enjoy the dollars I give you.

CHAVE

Since nothing is sinful to you, you lie like a horse
eats oats . . . not a penny of your money did I
touch— My poor daughter's torn fingers have kept
life in me . . . your dollars did educate your son,
but from the way he's carrying on, I don't see how
different it is from your business. . . .

THE SHAMES

I've raised my son to protect me and yet I'm not afraid to show my face to the world. Why do you sit under the counter all the time—is your face too beautiful for the world to see?

CHAVE

I don't want the world to see me in this robbers' den. . . .

[Zwi and Chono *appear near the pawnshop.*]

THE SHAMES

Heraus! Keep out! Don't you come in here or I'll have you arrested! Where's the rent?

ZWI

Here it is—may I come in now?

CHONO

Better take your shoes off first.

THE SHAMES

How much is it? The truth, now!

ZWI

Silver.

THE SHAMES

Are you making fun of me? You know how much the rent is!

CHONO AND ZWI

We collected and collected and that's all we could get.

THE SHAMES

The pockets inside out—hurry up!

CHONO (*to Zwi*)

You first!

THE SHAMES

Ah! Crooks!

[Zwi *takes out a couple of pieces of dry bread, a few spoons, a knife and a small bottle.*]

THE SHAMES

Now you! [CHONO *pulls out an assortment of eatables, nails, etc.*] That's all?

[Zwi *removes his hat and shows it to* THE SHAMES.]

CHONO

That's all, your majesty.

THE SHAMES

Before you're in the synagogue one hour I'll be there, too.

ZWI

Can we help it? It's your house and God's, and God hasn't paid rent . . .

CHONO

[*To* THE SHAMES.] Peace! [*As they walk off.*]
. . . and lots of trouble to you.

THE SHAMES

Now I've got to look for tenants.

CHAVE

Who's going to live in a place that was once a
house of worship?

THE SHAMES

I'll find the kind of people who don't believe in
that.

CHAVE

The lord will bless you for that.

THE SHAMES

A rich man doesn't need the lord's blessing, and
as for you, get out! Out! Where are you driving
me to, you snake? Tfu, tfu, on you! You make
me tremble with your snake talk! Oh, the hell with
this business and everything else! [*He closes the
doors of the shop . . . an old phonograph is grind-
ing the Kallarash dance out of its system.* FLOSSIE
*is singing: "All last night he called her Snooky
ookums."* . . . *A small room made up of screens*

. . . cheap drapery hides a bed . . . pictures; R.
the GIRL STRIKER *. . . opposite her is* FLOSSIE,
henna haired, dowdy, wrapped in a bright kimono.
Forming the other end of the triangle is ELKE, *who*
stands straight as a fir, her fingers interlocked
. . . her arms hanging limply, her speech is quiet,
gentle, soothing . . . while she is talking the drunken
FLOSSIE *makes a racket with her feet, claps her*
hands, whistles and sings.]

In the Brothel

ELKE

Is it not better, I say to you, as I've said to many
other young women . . . to be safe at home here,
instead of being burned up in a factory like those
other poor girls were . . . what I have to say to
you has much reason, for I am not young any more
and I have seen many sides of life . . . here you
can have whatever your heart desires . . . you may
save up much money . . . is it not so, Flossie?

FLOSSIE

The truth trickles from her mouth like honey
from a bee.

ELKE

You have been here long and you ought to know.

FLOSSIE

Don't I know it? Don't I? More than you think, Mother, more than you think.

ELKE

[*To* GIRL.] It is lucky that you are pretty and you are even luckier that we have room for you. If there is any vacancy my son always sees to it that it is filled.

FLOSSIE

Her son has a heart—it has more pity than a——
[*A warning finger from* ELKE *stops her.*]

ELKE

She is very jolly tonight . . . I believe in that . . . one should be jolly . . . not always, for there are times when one should give thought to the sad things of life, as my husband, Alter, olav hasholem, used to say. He was a holy man, and pure too, and there was no one like him . . . he was learned and he read the Talmud daily, except on Yom Kippur, when he fasted and said nothing but prayers . . . he always said to me: "Be charitable to the young, for they have not learned the ways of life yet and you must guide them!" . . . That is why I always go out of my way to help those who are young and come here seeking a home. . . .

FLOSSIE

[*Weeping.*] It was my bad luck to come here when I was already old. Oh, Mother Superior, if your heart gets fonder and fonder of the young flowers, what will happen to me? [*To the* GIRL.] To hell with the silver, to hell with the gold, oh, little sister, don't be bold!

ELKE

My son will take care of you.

FLOSSIE

[*Singing.*] Her son has soft fingers except on a gun!

ELKE

Hush! Nothing good will ever come of you!

FLOSSIE

Thunder and lightning, but that's the truth!

ELKE

My son has never harmed a fly . . . he gives much to charity.

FLOSSIE

Three cheers and bottoms up!

ELKE

You should take notice of this young woman who is your younger sister and cheer her up, for you can see that she is sad.

FLOSSIE

[*Singing.*] Hush, little sister, don't you cry, you'll get a man bye and bye!

ELKE

Many girls have married out of here and are very happy now. If I had a daughter! [*But she checks her tongue and then spits in a corner.*] I shall pray for you, child, and for you, too, Flossie!

FLOSSIE

[*Singing.*] Oh, Mother, put me to sleep with a prayer on my lip!

ELKE

You should pray for yourself. . . . Good night. [*Exits.*]

FLOSSIE

[*Offering the* GIRL *a drink.*] Have a drink or have it not, there goes the banker with his pot! Whatchu cryin' for, little one? This ain't the gutter youse had hoid sky pilots bark about . . . no, no . . . only soldiers and cripples is in the gutter . . .

here we don't have to beg . . . we get it. . . .
[*Singing.*] Hush, little sister, don't you cry, you'll
get a man bye and bye!

In the Synagogue

CHONO

[*In a loud voice.*] Wake up, or you'll fall asleep!

ZWI

I haven't fallen asleep, so I don't have to wake
up.

[*In the synagogue* ZWI *and* CHONO *are seen
stretched out on the floor.*]

ZWI

[*Produces a little mirror from his pocket and examines his tongue.*] It's green.

CHONO

When a man does not eat, his tongue gets the
color of his dreams and your dreams are green.

ZWI

Why are they green?

CHONO

Because you were born in the country and, like a
cow, dream of pasture.

ZWI

Ah, that . . . that is true . . . ah, the country
is beautiful now . . . now is the time they cut hay
. . . ah, the odor of new hay . . . ah . . . ah . . . and
the kvass . . . rivers of it . . . and the girls we
used to kiss and the pranks we played. . . . I sometimes curse the Rabbis who concocted the Talmud
so that I would have to spend my life trying to figure
it out . . . but what is that to you, born in a synagogue and dreaming of nothing but funerals, angels
and dried apples?

CHONO

Better than dreaming of dried women and grass
and cows.

ZWI

Ah, but I could eat a dinner now and drink a
glass of . . . mmmmmmmmmmmmmm . . . but where
can we get it? That's a question you've never an-
swered me since we've held up the roof of this synagogue and yet you're as hungry as myself. I believe the devil helps you out a bit . . . in fact, I did
smell a little sulphur here last night. . . .

CHONO

It's easy for you to joke, but my head aches.

ZWI

Why shouldn't it ache—it's a good head.

CHONO

It isn't good any more—it's been used up trying
to figure out why the Shames, with a face that
would shame a Tartar and with as much wisdom as
a dead crow, can come to America and get so rich
that he owns a street, this synagogue, and you and
me.

ZWI

I wouldn't look at the problem with spectacles,
Chono . . . it's plain that the Shames is not too
anxious to go to heaven . . . that's all.

CHONO

For a good meal and a bed, I'd give up heaven
too. [*Footsteps are heard.*] Shshshshsh, who can
that be?

ZWI

Perhaps it's the Shames, olav hasholem.

CHONO

Why do you say olav hasholem when he isn't
dead yet?

ZWI

When a man passes me every morning and never
gives me a penny, he might as well be dead.

CHONO

Nu, in that case the synagogue is closed to the dead. [*Locks the door.*]

ZWI

What does he want now, rent again?

CHONO

We haven't paid him rent since we've been here, and still he wants rent. Where will we get the rent?

ZWI

Not from me, not from you.

CHONO

It's landlord's business to ask for rent and it's our business not to pay it . . . that settles it. . . . [*Knocking on door. Pause.*] Say, maybe they want to pray . . . there may be a meal in those customers. . . .

ZWI

Nu, open the door then. . . . [*They open the door slowly and immediately their stock phrase is on its way.*]

ZWI AND CHONO

A penny . . . penny . . . penny . . . pennny . . . a penny . . . a penny . . . a penny.

THE SHAMES

[*Walks in.*] A penny, eh? A penny? You sing well, but the wrong tune! Have you got a bed here? No. Have you got a closet here? No. Is this your home? No. Have you paid rent? No. Then I've got to tell you that you aren't here any more. I have new tenants for this place and they have rent and they know how to honor a landlord—heraus! Run and tell the Rabbi and the congregation that my word is so! Nu, run!

CHONO

If I had a place to run to, I'd run, but as I haven't, so why should I run at all?

THE SHAMES

Run and tell them my words! [CHONO *skips out.*] Tonight the new tenants move in. I am going. [*Exits.*]

ZWI

Go! Am I holding you back? Even unto fire and flood and destruction may you go and then I won't hold you back . . . nu, the old home is going the way of all Israel . . . [*Collects his things and stuffs them in a bag.*]

In the Brothel

FLOSSIE'S VOICE

Hush, little sister, don't you cry, you'll get a man, bye and bye! [*We get a glimpse of the whore house room. . . . FLOSSIE . . . reeling . . . looks around.*] Jesus, where in the hell did that goil go to? [*Moves up stage and looks down . . . with a sudden cry.*] There she is! Jesus! Jumped out! Holy Mary! [*Reeling back to her seat.*] The hell with her . . . more chance for me . . . this woild ain't big enough for old and young. . . . [*Loud police whistle.*] Jesus, that bitch has gone to the devil sure!

In the Synagogue.

RABBI'S VOICE

[*From the synagogue.*] For the place that lies desolate . . .

CONGREGATION

We sit in solitude and mourn!

RABBI

For the temple that was destroyed . . .

CONGREGATION

We sit in solitude and mourn!

RABBI

For the walls that are overthrown . . .

CONGREGATION

We sit in solitude and mourn!

RABBI

For our majesty that is departed . . .

CONGREGATION

We sit in solitude and mourn!

RABBI

[*Crescendo.*] For our great who lie dead . . .

CONGREGATION

[*Crescendo.*] We sit in solitude and mourn!

RABBI

For the precious stones that lie buried.

CONGREGATION

We sit in solitude and mourn.

RABBI

We sit in solitude and mourn.

CONGREGATION

We sit in solitude and mourn.

RABBI

We sit in solitude and mourn . . . we sit in
solitude and mourn . . . O Israel, thy house is falling down . . . what is thy answer to this, O Israel?
Thou sayest thou art in America . . . thou sayest
that this is a new land . . . that thou livest in new
centuries, but I say unto thee, that there are no
new lands . . . no new periods . . . no new ways
for thee . . . what does Israel want with new modes
. . . it is the same today as it was yesterday, as it
will be tomorrow. [*Suddenly cries out.*] The word
to thee is this, Israel: They who do not come unto
me I shall discard! [*With fury.*] My curses will
fall upon you all like hail from the sky! There will
be no escape for thee! Bring the candles! Light the
candles! Blow the Shafers! [*Covering himself with
the "Talisch"—prayer cloth—his hands outstretched before him, he rushes wildly to the closet
where the scrolls are kept. There we hear him
gushing forth, while the* CONGREGATION *files out non-
chalantly.* THE SHAMES *comes in with* REUBEN;
*the latter is holding a roll of paper in his hand
. . . the* RABBI *turns front again without seeing the
intruders . . . his hands raised above him, tears
streaming from his eyes, his voice shrill and sharp.*]

RABBI

Bring down fire and brimstone upon this city of

iniquity! They have left thy house to rot and to pass into the hands of strangers! Here are the names of the men. [*Turns slowly and sees his enemies.*]

THE SHAMES

[*Quickly.*] It is time to go, Rabbi . . . we are going to clean this place up . . . the new tenants are here! Your friends, the strikers, will make this their home. [*In a fit of fury and madness the* RABBI *rends his garments and falls upon the floor.*]

RABBI

Is this the first sign of the passing of Israel as a people?

REUBEN

They are weary travelers who have found a home at last . . . the house is bare, but for vermin and rodents, but for vampires and owls. We are cleaning the house . . . the neighbors shout insults at us . . . they say we are destroying the house, but we sweep on, heeding none, for we are the storm that is blowing to all the corners of the earth. . . .

RABBI

Then step down from your mountain, Moses . . . step down . . . where is there now a stone I may call my own, or a wall I may lean against . . . the

sun is beyond the clouds and I've hidden my eyes so
as not to see the ruin of my house . . . let me die
here . . . I am the symbol of the end of Israel . . .
just let me stay here long enough to say the funeral
service for a dead race: "Ishakadal v'ishkadash
shmai rabbo!"

[REUBEN *hangs up a large sign* "THERE IS NO
GOD" . . . *the* RABBI *ends the service.*]

REUBEN

. . . to all the corners of the earth . . .
[*The* PICKETS *march on.*]

CHORUS OF MEN PICKETS

. . . to all the corners of the earth . . .

CHORUS OF WOMEN PICKETS

. . . to all the corners of the earth . . .

FULL CHORUS OF PICKETS

. . . to all the corners of the earth . . .

THE CURTAIN CLOSES

FIFTH ACT

Panorama for the damned——*Pity the thirsty*
sea——*The Earth is sterile*——*"Mazol Tov"*——
Electricity is Peace——*Exodus.*

* * * * * * *

[*Over the pawnshop is a sign "Jake Finkel Demo-*
cratic Club." The curtains part to a chorus which
at times sounds like the croaking of bullfrogs; then
suddenly changes tone and suggests a line of 'cellos
holding a festival all by themselves . . . the instru-
ments are human voices . . . voices of old men
and women . . . beggars and the RABBI *. . . hoarse,*
shrill, plaintive and forlorn. . . . The pickets march
on wearily . . . slowly . . . circle the stage and march
off.]

CHORUS

Pity the poor . . . pity the poor . . . pity the
poor . . . pity the poor . . . pity the poor. . . .

FIRST BEGGAR

[*The* FIRST OLD IMMIGRANT.]
Bread for the living . . . pity the poor. . . .

178

Pity the poor . . . pity the poor . . . pity the
poor. . . .

I am cold . . . there is no sun today and that
is why I am cold. . . .

You've been saying that for weeks and yet the
sun is out . . . there is the sun!

Pity the poor . . . there is no sun . . . I can
see no sun. . . .

You are blind and so cannot see the sun and do
not believe others. . . .

I can see no sun, and what I do not see I do not
believe . . . pity the poor . . . besides, there are
no days and nights here . . . the noises, the lights
and the people are always the same . . . the moon
comes when the sun should and the sun waits . . .
I am cold. . . .

It is strange . . . strange . . . I've sat here all
day long and received nothing . . . when my

daughter, olav hasholem, was alive, I did not have to wait all day long for my piece of bread. . . .

SECOND BEGGAR

But I have a son and he is alive and yet I must beg. . . .

FIRST BEGGAR

There are stories coming here from that city where the great lights shine that there is little bread there.

WOMAN BEGGAR

My daughter worked there, too.

FIRST BEGGAR

They also say that there is no work . . . bad times have come . . . there is a strike, but I do not know what that means . . . new things come into the world and one does not know what they mean . . . it is terrible to be old. . . .

SECOND BEGGAR

But the news may not be true . . . my son also told me that he is a striker and has not worked in months, but many lies are told to the poor and old, and more lies to cover the first lies, and thus do the liars achieve peace . . . pity the poor . . . did you not tell me once that you had a son?

FIRST BEGGAR

Yes, but he is a great man and it is not seemly for an old beggar of a father to shame him by his presence. . . .

SECOND BEGGAR

Is he not in New York?

FIRST BEGGAR

Yes . . . is it far away, this city of New York?

SECOND BEGGAR

I always thought that this was New York.

FIRST BEGGAR

No, no, this is called Hester.

WOMAN BEGGAR

Hester Street. . . .

FIRST BEGGAR

That is too long a name for my tongue . . . when they took me off the boat, they put me in a closed wagon and I couldn't see where I was going and I have never seen that city called New York . . . we talked much about it when we were young . . . it must be a strange city . . . a wonderful city and it is a terrible feeling that one must die without

seeing it . . . I've heard that there are millions of
people there . . . millions . . . they are all very rich
and have many wives and drink very strong liquors,
stronger even than the hundred proof vodka that
the peasants drank in the old world . . . it is terrible to die without seeing so great a city . . . terrible. . . . [*Pause.*]   Have mercy on an old man
. . . have mercy. . . .

CHORUS

Pity the poor . . . pity the poor . . . pity the
poor. . . .

SECOND BEGGAR

I asked my son once to take me there, but he said
that the city was built by the young for the young
and the old are not swift or sure enough of their
limbs to walk their streets . . . he also told me
that there are buildings that reach to the skies, but
I do not believe that, for in the town of my birth
there was a rich man who built a mansion of *four*
stories and the Rabbi forbade people to go into it,
or even pass within its shadow, for he said that it
would fall when the devil was in the wind . . . how,
then, can they have buildings that go up to the
skies when the winds here are stronger, for we are
near great water . . . pity a homeless man . . .
pity. . . .

CHORUS

Pity the poor . . . pity the poor . . . pity the poor. . . .

FIRST BEGGAR

But it is terrible to die without seeing so strange a city. . . .

WOMAN BEGGAR

My daughter did see it and did die and what glory did she get and what compensation have I of it?

SECOND BEGGAR

True . . . true . . . but is it not more terrible to die in a strange land when all my life long I dreamed of dying in Jerusalem? . . . [*Sings.*] Yerusholaem, O Yerusholaem!

FIRST BEGGAR

[*Dreamily.*] If my eyes would become little birds and fly away from me to that wonderful city and look in the windows, at the people, the streets, and all the marvelous things that youth has built for itself . . . if my eyes would only become little birds . . . but they are like birds that have no wings and so stay within my body as in a nest that is cold and bare . . . while that great city goes on . . . pity the poor . . . a little charity . . . mercy. . . I am cold . . . mercy. . . .

SECOND BEGGAR

Here's some snuff: this is the beginning and the end of my charity and mercy.

WOMAN BEGGAR

She did see the wonderful city and she did die and what glory is there to her, to me, or the city . . . pity the poor. . . .

CHORUS

Pity the poor . . . pity the poor . . . pity the poor. . . .

> [ELKE *emerges from the darkness and approaches the* BEGGARS, *depositing coins and small packages in their laps.*]

ELKE

Pray . . . pray for my son and let your prayers be heard in heaven. . . .

FIRST BEGGAR

What are the prayers of strange beggars to the prayers of a mother?

ELKE

My prayers will not be heard for my name is no more on the roll of names . . . nor is the name of my son. . . .

SECOND BEGGAR

What is thy name and what is the name of thy son?

ELKE

Abomination.

WOMAN BEGGAR

No, no . . . for have you not given us much money now and food . . . you are a blessing . . . !

ELKE

Abomination thrives . . . while the whole city is starving and the children look into the hungry eyes of their mothers, a mother thrives on the sins of her son. . . . I would run, but the road is black in the day as in the night, but the end must come, for has it not been said that there is an end to everything? [*Walks off haltingly towards the saloon.*]

FIRST BEGGAR

How can the kind and charitable be so sinful? It is a strange world, this new one we've been brought to . . . strange. . . .

SECOND BEGGAR

Everything new is strange. . . . [*Pause.*] There is enough in this bundle for a feast. . . . What are you doing, Menashe?

FIRST BEGGAR

Preparing for my meal. . . .

SECOND BEGGAR

But you must not wash your hands in the gutter. . . .

FIRST BEGGAR

There is no other water for those who sit upon the ground. . . . [*They eat.*]

YOSHKE

[*Meeting* ELKE *in front of the saloon.*]
Keep an eye open for Yankel and Louis.

ELKE

What's happening?

YOSHKE

Double-crossin' me . . . double-crossin' me. . . .
[*Reënters saloon* . . . ELKE *throws coins to the beggars.*]

ELKE

Pray for us . . . pray for us! [*Goes back to her place.*]

CHORUS

Mmmmmmmmmmm . . . mmmm . . . mmmmmmm. . . .

RABBI

[*A beaten figure now . . . his rabbinical garb torn . . . shoes unlaced . . . bosom bare.*] Where is your house . . . the house that stands on quicksand . . . the house that boasts of its iniquities . . . where is it? Ah, but there she stands, like a tower braving the wind . . . nay, daughter of Sodom, to escape me you must go higher than the clouds, for I've weighed the weights, and measured the measures, and I know the sum that belongs to the victor, and the debt that is due me . . . daughter of Sodom, hear my voice . . . count the pennies in the right hand for the virgins that you despoiled and count the pennies in the left hand for the youth——

ELKE

[*Faintly.*] Hush, Rabbi,—hush . . . only yesterday I gave you money for food and drink and now you speak evil of me again . . . here! [*Hands him money.*]

RABBI

May thy children and thy children's children and thy goats and thy land increase until the end of the world, when judgment comes! Forgive an old man, virtuous woman, for he is but a tree stump; neither rain nor sun nor wind can raise it to the skies, nor can it give shade to the weary traveler, but it must cling to the earth like a worm: why, then, mind the words of a worm? But I must mind the words of the sages who said that on Purim you should get so drunk that you cannot tell the difference between Mordecai hung Haman and Haman hung Mordecai and all *my* days are Purim days. . . . [*Gets up, walking off.*] Haman hung Mordecai, Mordecai hung Haman! [*Stops in front of the pawnshop.*] Where is the Shames, the despoiler of my temple . . . where is he who sold my house for a few shakels? . . . But in hell thy gold and silver will melt away and what is left thee no crows will ever look upon! Mordecai hung . . . [*Scampers off.* . . .]

CHORUS

[*Praying.*] Mmmmm . . . mmmmm . . . mmmmm.
[*A cold light, blue and gray, finds* Zwi *and* Chono *asleep on a stairway . . . the cold morning air tickles them and they wake up.*]

ZWI

Hard . . . the books in the synagogue made a softer bed—we lived there a long time, eh, Chono?

CHONO

A long time . . . I had nine teeth then, now I have only three.

ZWI

Three? You lie, you have one more hidden away somewhere in your mouth. Always cheating. . . . Brrr, I'm hungry . . . hungry. . . .

CHONO

I'm twice as hungry. . . . It's really cold . . . brrrr. . . winter is coming and where are we going to spend our night then, eh?

ZWI

He's thinking of winter and I'm thinking of the future!

CHONO

Aha, what future is that? [*Pause.*] Getting old, ha? Aha! Time to think of the future!

ZWI

Say it! You can say it with three teeth too . . . time to think of green grass, eh? [*Look at each other closely and then turn away.*] Green grass grows on the top of the ground. . . . [*Produces a picture from his pocket and shows it to his partner.*] See the picture? See it? They got four new plots there . . . four. . . .

CHONO

What's the name of the—cemetery?

ZWI

That's Mount Zion . . . looks like it's not too noisy.

CHONO

No, it's quiet . . . nice thick grass, but the trees arc too small. . . .

ZWI

[*Bitterly.*]   Young trees. . . .

CHONO

Is Mount Zion in Canarsie?

ZWI

It is, but the ground is full of gravel.

CHONO

That's not very good, but still Reb Simon is resting there . . . peace to him. . . .

ZWI

Peace to him. . . .

CHONO

My wife, Shore, is resting there, peace to her!

ZWI

Peace to her! Then it would not be proper for you to go to another place.

CHONO

But she was my second wife . . . my third wife is in Haves Sachem.

ZWI

There are rocks there and the ground is moist.

CHONO

Rocks may keep the ground moist, but the diggers always pull them out first, otherwise they can't dig.

ZWI

Your wisdom is like a lamp going dry . . . it smokes but gives no light . . . the rocks are there just the same and I won't go there!

CHONO

What? What did you say? Ai, ai, ai, ai, my best friend will go to a strange place! Zwi, may worms dance a kasatski on your head if you go there! Do not go there, Zwi . . . promise me you won't go there . . . we lived together so many years, don't let us separate in death . . . I plead with you . . . I'll drag you with me . . . I'll come and disturb your sleep . . . promise me you won't go there . . . promise me . . . do you hear me? [*But* Zwi *has fallen asleep.*] Ah, sleep . . . you always sleep when you're hungry—when that's the time to go out begging food. Wake up, Zwi, and let's go to the Shames's house; he may give us some of the cake from the wedding . . . do you hear me? [*They walk off*, CHONO *leading*.]

In the Club

[YANKEL *is in his club room: the* CAPTAIN *rushes in.*]

CAPTAIN

Jake, we pinched Yoshke for butcherin' and bumpin' off strikers on the picket line against orders, and then had to let him go. It's gettin' us in a hell of a fix.

YANKEL

Why?

CAPTAIN

He was gonna squeal on the graft in this precinct and if any more of that gets to the boss, we're cooked. He's got to go . . . this time there's no foolin' about it. He and his gang's got to move on. You got to do it, Jake, an' we don't want this business to get in the papers. Things ain't run the old way no more . . . somethin' happened. Don't know what. Maybe it's them starvin' rats. . . . Jesus, lemme catch my breath . . . them rats is goin' to win that strike sure and they say the gangsters got to go. If Yoshke snitches on us . . . Jake, he's got to go. Make a clean job of it . . . no poipers, no court. Use his own gang for that.

YANKEL

All right.   Scare up Louis and bring him here.

CAPTAIN

We got him spotted.   [*Leaves quickly.*]

CHORUS

[*Praying.*]   Mmmmm . . . mmmmm . . . mmmmm.

In the Saloon

YOSHKE

[*To* ELKE.]   Did you hear the police whistles?
There's a lot of bulls around here.   Somethin's goin'
to happen.   I wish I'd listened to you and moved
to the Bronx.

ELKE

Why can't we do it now?

YOSHKE

All right—pack up!

In the Club

LOUIS

[*Entering the club room.*]   Say, Yankel, what's
the idea of this roundin' up business?   Say, I don't
take orders with me mits in de air . . . I got them
in me pocket, get me?

YANKEL

Cut the hero stuff.   There's orders that takes you
in, too.   I'm making it easy for you . . . you take

my orders or . . . pluggin' me won't do you no
good. Take them mits out of your pocket . . . you
ain't got the drop on me this time . . . my orders
is : watch out Yoshke don't skip . . . if he does he'll
be on the run . . . if he snitches . . .

LOUIS

I tell you, Jake, he ain't goin' to snitch. . . .

YANKEL

I know better . . . been tipped off . . . why the
hell do you think they let him go after he plugged
a striker? . . . he sure snitched . . . there's been
gangs of dicks here lamping the place . . . if
Yoshke coughs any more, you're going to fry sure
and plenty . . . he's got to go, Louis. . . .

LOUIS

Jesus . . . I dunno . . . Jesus, Yankle, don't get
me to do the big job. I ain't had no fun in life yet.
Don't let me fry. . . . Say, Jake, you ain't goin' to
double-cross me?

YANKEL

Hell, no . . . if you're with me, Louis, I'll give
you a good berth . . . see if I don't . . . he's got
to go or we all go . . . I got more brains than he
and we can run the whole push by ourselves . . .
watch out, Lou, there's a guy blockin' . . .

LOUIS

Nope, that's my rib on the look-out . . . Jesus,
Jake, you ain't got me trapped, have youse?

YANKEL

What the hell makes you think that?

LOUIS

I ain't sure of nobody now. . . .

YANKEL

There they go, Louis. . . .
   [*A man skulks past the shop and whistles
   . . .* LOUIS *echoes it . . . a second man comes
   on and the procedure is repeated.* LOUIS
   whispers to his men.]

LOUIS

Sure goin' to stand by me, Jake?

YANKEL

[*Sotto voce.*] I'm with you . . . go ahead. . . .
   [LOUIS *stalks out . . . suddenly there is a
   shot . . . then another . . . then a third
   . . . three men run off in various directions
   . . .* YOSHKE *is seen falling . . . gun in hand
   . . . a policeman runs on . . . examines*

YOSHKE's *body, pulls out billy, pounds side-*
walk, blows whistle, pulls out gun, looks
about . . . and dashes off . . . echoing police
whistles are heard . . . from nooks and cor-
ners bent and wizened old BEGGARS *shuffled on,*
looking like some unearthly vultures, tin cups
in their hands, handkerchiefs spread over
their palms, chanting. . . .]

On the Street

BEGGARS

Chdoko tachil mmoves . . . charity will save you
from death . . . chdoko tachil mmoves. . . .
 [ELKE *rushes to the body of her son and, fall-*
 ing before it, begins to force the BEGGARS *off,*
 but they return again and again.]

ELKE

Pity . . . pity . . . nothing but pity! The ocean
drinking itself . . . pity . . . charity . . . he gave
much charity, but that did not save him from death
. . . Eili eili lomo azavtoni! Away, ghouls! He
was my abomination and my charity! If he sinned,
he was still my son! If I gave birth to him, so do
you all give birth to six lawyers to defend him, a
fence to buy the fruit of his deeds, a judge to be
bribed and now a grave digger to bury him . . .
away, vultures! I shall close his eyes myself . . .

I shall fold his arms. . . . [*One by one the* BEGGARS *sink to the ground, muttering a prayer.*]

In the Club

DETECTIVE

[*A* DETECTIVE *brings in* LOUIS.] Nice day, ain't it, Louis?

LOUIS

Yeah—fine.

DETECTIVE

Clancy caught him on the corner, his gat's got one missing.

LOUIS

You know me, boys. What's the idea? What's up?

CAPTAIN

[*With deference due a professional criminal.*] Say, Louis, what do you know about the Shtarker business? You an' him was thick, wasn't you?

LOUIS

Nothin' . . . I was in Joisy with my mother all day and just came in when Clancy grabs me. It's ok this time, Cap, I had nothin' to do with it.

CAPTAIN

Better come clean with it, Louis; the new Commish is as hard as nails and he wants the goods

brought in or there'll be hell to pay for someone.
[*He consults* YANKEL.] Sorry, Louis, but we got
to hold you. . . .

LOUIS

Say, Cap, I got to get a square deal sometime
. . . there ain't nothin' on me, you know it yourself. . . .

CAPTAIN

Sorry, Louis . . . clip . . . fourteen Mac . . .
eyes open . . . call the wagon.

LOUIS

If somebody's double-crossed me, I'll get even with
him. . . .
[*The* DETECTIVES *move off with* LOUIS . . . *the
stage has been cleared of the previous scene.
Several women are standing on stairways
. . . fire-escapes or looking through windows.* ELKE *is moving out . . . moving men
are carrying out bundles . . .* ELKE *is standing in front of her house . . . long
pause. . . .*]

On the Stairs

FIRST WOMAN

Go on, skip away . . . we see you . . . **go on**
and hurry . . . drag yourself away. . . .

SECOND WOMAN

Many years you lived here and gave us nothing but shame and disgrace. . . .

THIRD WOMAN

Where you moving to: the grave?

FOURTH WOMAN

No, to the Bronx . . . there are fine homes there . . . new ones . . . there are no roaches . . . no rats to bite your babies. . . .

FIFTH WOMAN

There's parks there . . . parks . . . trees and flowers and grass and shade. . . .

FIRST WOMAN

Why should she go there—she ain't desoived it. . . .

SECOND WOMAN

Let her go to hell—our children will be safe now . . . tear her eyes out, so she won't see her new home?

THIRD WOMAN

Break her bones for her! Why should she be lucky like that and we have to stay here! [*Incipient mêlée,* VLADISLAV *comes to* ELKE'S *defense.*]

VLADISLAV

[*To* ELKE.] I been here fifteen years or more
. . . forgot how long . . . so long . . . I feel it
is a long time . . . long time . . . all alone all the
time . . . all alone . . . Jesus, I feel too much
alone . . . terrible feeling, oh, how terrible . . . I
don't know nobody . . . I ain't got no friends . . .
a big country but no people . . . no people . . .
Jesus, I feel lonely, there are no women like in the
old country . . . no woman to marry . . . no woman
. . . I like to go out and say hello to somebody and
have a drink and sing a song and do a dance, but
there are no people . . . no people at all . . . some
day I go away from here . . . I run away somewhere . . . Jesus, but I am lonely . . . I like to say
good night to somebody . . . I . . . [*Pause.*] You
going away?—oh, good-by. Some day come back
—come back, yes? Goodby.

ELKE

[*Walks off with moving men.*] Good-by, good-
by . . . !

 [VLADISLAV *wipes a tear and goes down to his
 basement.* REUBEN *and* GITEL *and the*
 PICKETS *march on again.*]

GITEL

This strike has been like a storm to this place . . .
everything is dead . . . the little grocery stores are
empty . . . the children do not play any more—
there's no music . . . life is waiting . . . waiting. . . .

REUBEN

But the sweatshop kings are not rejoicing, either
. . . they are giving way, little by little . . . they
have granted most of our demands, but we'll fight
on until we win a complete victory. . . .

GITEL

But how long will the weary pickets have to march
on . . . how long will the children have to wait for
their food . . . how long will this agony of waiting . . . waiting . . . last? [*Suddenly.*] Reuben,
let us announce the latest offer from the bosses
. . . we two can wait, but they . . . let them hear
the new offers and pass upon them. . . .

REUBEN

Perhaps you are right . . . you feel this more
poignantly than I, for you see more and sense more.
. . . [*Gets up on the stairway.*] There are three
new offers: Piece work . . .

PICKETS

[*Almost in a hush.*] No.

REUBEN

Fifty-two hour week . . .

PICKETS

[*Stronger.*] No.

REUBEN

Same old shops . . .

PICKETS

[*A mighty shout.*] No! No! NO!
  [*The march becomes more enervating and
  faster as they go off.*]

FOURTH WOMAN

[*Dreamily.*] Sunshine . . . trees . . . new homes
. . . you can raise children there. . . .

FIFTH WOMAN

What's the use of raising children here . . . and
you're going to have another one, too.

FOURTH WOMAN

None of your business!

FIFTH WOMAN

Your husband hasn't worked for months: your children are starved!

FOURTH WOMAN

Shut your mouth! Wipe your nose first before you talk to decent people. You're boiling over yourself, because you got too many children and got to live here!

FIFTH WOMAN

That so? If I wanted to, I could move out right now!

FOURTH WOMAN

What you got to move out,—two saucers and a leaky pot?

FIFTH WOMAN

That's more than you ever had . . . when you first came here we had to give you salt.

FOURTH WOMAN

Give me back my frying pan!

FIFTH WOMAN

You got nothin' to fry in it, anyway—you can't fry bones!

FOURTH WOMAN

Oh, kiss my—you know!

FIFTH WOMAN

I'll choke you foist!

FOURTH WOMAN

There is a garbage can; pick out your dinner, you starving rat!

FIFTH WOMAN

Insult me, go on, insult me! Keep right on! [*Bursts out crying. . . .*]

FIRST WOMAN

What did you have to hurt her for—haven't **we** got enough trouble as it is? [*The* FOURTH WOMAN *tries to calm the* FIFTH.]

FOURTH WOMAN

I am sorry . . . I didn't mean to hurt you . . . it's misery that makes us quarrel like that . . . misery . . . we all have plenty of it . . . when the strike is over, things will be better. . . .

FIFTH WOMAN

If the strike will ever come to an end . . . if it ever will . . . you can keep the frying pan . . . I . . . I have nothing to fry in it . . . nothing. . . . [*She goes up to her flat . . . the rest remain in their places, mute, stony, visionless . . . the* FIFTH WOMAN *is in her flat . . . her* HUSBAND *is in a corner.*]

In a Flat

FIFTH WOMAN

I've carried your brood in my belly long enough
. . . I've given birth to seven children. Where is
the bread for your seven children? Bread . . .
there will be no more children . . . no more . . .
not from me . . . all night long I've walked to kill
that which is in my belly . . . I've stamped my feet
on the hard sidewalks . . . I've pressed my body
against the sharp corners of buildings . . . bread
for those who are already born. . . .

THE HUSBAND

Where shall I get you bread?

FIFTH WOMAN

Go out and beg . . . steal. . . .

THE HUSBAND

Didn't I go out yesterday to sell my last clothes?

FIFTH WOMAN

[*Eagerly.*] Where is the money? Where is the
bread?

THE HUSBAND

They gave me a quarter for it. . . .

FIFTH WOMAN

WHERE IS THE BREAD?

THE HUSBAND

They said the quarter was counterfeit and they
gave me no bread for it, but cursed me and it is
awful to curse a father and a husband . . . so I
threw the quarter away. . . . [*Long pause.*]

FIFTH WOMAN

So this is the period of prosperity . . . yes, for
the druggist . . . for the doctor . . . the under-
taker . . . the grave digger. . . .

THE HUSBAND

But the grave digger is also a worker. . . .
[*Pause.*]

FIFTH WOMAN

Go out and see if you can get a little whiskey
. . . I will give the children a few teaspoons . . .
that will put them to sleep—for it is horrible to be
hungry and to be awake. . . .

THE HUSBAND

I do not want to go . . . for there is always the
fear in me that I will go away . . . far away from
my children and you . . . for my pity is stronger
than my reason . . . I do not want to go. . . .
[*The* FIFTH WOMAN *moves down and stands limply*

. . . THE HUSBAND *continues soothingly and reminiscently.*] My hands were never idle . . . well you know it . . . at home before I learned the agony of the factory needle, one summer I received for my labor six bushels of corn . . . ten sacks of potatoes . . . nine ducks . . . my share for my labor. . . .

FIFTH WOMAN

The thrashing . . . the honey . . . stuff the ducks and sew them up with white thread—the summer is not too warm . . . the sun is kind . . . the earth fruitful . . . but the song of the wind is America . . . the dancers step to the tune of America . . . the dream at sundown and the dream at sunset is America. . . . [*Cries out.*] Gold! The streets are paved with gold! Gold is freedom . . . gold is peace . . . gold is salvation——

On the Stairs

FIRST WOMAN

Eat the gold, then . . . feed it to your children. . . .

SECOND WOMAN

Eat freedom . . . eat salvation . . . eat peace . . . .

THIRD WOMAN

I have bitten into my heart to make it still. . . .

FOURTH WOMAN

I want to cry out, but I can't . . . I want to curse all creation, but my tongue is dry. . . .

FIFTH WOMAN

I am as dry as sand that's been abused by the sun and beaten by the wind. . . .

FIRST WOMAN

If one could lift one's children high . . . high . . . and save them from your eyes. . . .

SECOND WOMAN

Wherever your children go, your eyes go. . . .

THIRD WOMAN

It is horrible to have both eyes and children. . . .

FOURTH WOMAN

He learns to walk and he learns to hunger . . . he learns to talk and he learns to hunger. . . .

FIFTH WOMAN

I walked the streets all night to kill that which is within me . . . there is enough . . . enough. . . .

CHORUS OF WOMEN

The seed of the corn planted in the ground . . . the seed of the rye . . . of oats . . . the harvests

. . . the song of the harvests . . . the fruit of the
soil . . . the earth is not sterile . . . the earth is
fruitful . . . *where is the harvest?* . . . where is
the *fruit?* . . . the earth is potent . . . there is the
seed . . . *where is the harvest? where is the fruit?*

FIFTH WOMAN

There are enough worlds . . . let us hide our
children before they are born . . . it is time to
plunder the heart of every sentiment and feeling
for there is nothing left. . . .

FIRST WOMAN

You are given death before life. . . .

SECOND WOMAN

When a child is born, whole worlds are born. . . .

THIRD WOMAN

But they are dead worlds . . . death before
life. . . .

FOURTH WOMAN

His mother is but an evil wind caressing and leav-
ing him to pass on. . . .

FIFTH WOMAN

I walked all night to kill that which is struggling
to come to life, for the earth has become sterile

. . . god has gone to seed . . . god is sterile . . .
the earth has gone to seed. . . .

> [*The* PICKETS *drag themselves on, leaning on
> each other for support. Some leave the line
> and rest on the stairways or curbstones . . .
> suddenly* GITEL *and* REUBEN *appear in the
> former synagogue.*]

In Headquarters

REUBEN

Here is the latest offer: Forty-eight hours—**no**
piece work—new shops—VOTE! Forty-eight hours!

CHORUS

Yes?!

REUBEN

No piece work.

CHORUS

Yes!

REUBEN

New shops.

CHORUS

Yes, yes, yes!!!

REUBEN AND GITEL

The strike is over!

GITEL

The strike is over!

WE WIN!

MAN STRIKER

The strike is over!

WOMAN STRIKER

It is over. The strike is over!

MAN STRIKER

The strike is over.

ALL

We win, we win, we win!

A GIRL STRIKER

We win! [*Bursts out crying.*] We win! We win!

> [*By slow degrees the strikers begin to realize that they have achieved victory . . . they seem to be coming out of a long sleep . . . far away the machines are tuning up . . . the workers begin a pantomimic dance . . . slowly and sharply they describe in the air their reunion with the machines . . . the factory is coming to life . . . the machines become louder and more insistent . . . the workers dance off and are seen at the machines.*]

THE MACHINES

[*With triumphant exultation.*] Whirrrrrrr!!!
Whirrrrrrr! Whirrrrrrr!

NEWSBOYS

[*Running on.*] Extra, strike is won! Extra,
strike is won! Strike is over!

FIRST PHONOGRAPH

[*Plays second part of Sher dance.*]

SECOND PHONOGRAPH

[*Plays a joyful Jewish song.*]

THIRD PHONOGRAPH

[*Plays: "It ain't goin' to rain no more."*]
  [*Night is approaching . . . in one flat candles
  are being lit . . . the atmosphere is festive
  . . . the women are dressed in holiday attire
  . . . from the other flats, too, come music,
  light, song . . . the former synagogue is
  dimly lit and we see two figures at opposite
  sides of the room:* GITEL *and* REUBEN.]

REUBEN

Look, they are celebrating . . . the stores are re-
opening . . . the people are selling and buying

things . . . there is light and music . . . hearts are gay now . . . the sweat shops are gone . . . it means life again . . .

GITEL

We battled against the sweatshops. We lived on the picket line and in halls all that time. . . . Although my love for the machine and the shirtwaist is not stronger now than it was before, still, marching into conquered shops will give birth to new life, new forces within me. . . . I've been born again.

REUBEN

We have learned during these months much more than all the schools could have taught us. . . .

GITEL

I, too, have learned much since I've been in this country: bread earned by your own hands is sweet . . . that is enough for me . . . Reuben . . . I have a great dream: it is your dream, too:—I want to hold up a torch so that man may see in the dark . . . so that he may see the road . . . the clear and level road that lies before him . . . a light so strong that it will blind all those who do not want to see . . . that is our dream . . . I shall learn to be a mother to a dream . . . how to rear, nurse and bring it to full life. . . . As a part of our victory, Yoshke is no more. His heir, my brother, is marrying ten thousand dollars tonight and is getting a woman with it in the bargain . . . she will only be his dead wife, for blood and money trickle side by side in his veins . . . and money is love and life to him . . . he will betray, condemn, kill for his love . . . his dead wife will bear him many children with the stamp of the law on their foreheads, who will become mayors of Scum, Mud and Filth Streets. . . . [*Pause.*] I, too, shall be married tonight . . . I, too, shall have children. . . .

REUBEN

My mother had six children . . . she would cut six slices of bread and distribute them with eyes closed, for that was the beginning and the end of the meal . . . she took the loaves of bread out of the oven long before they were fully baked, so that they would be heavy and our bellies would fill up much quicker . . . in the summer heat our bellies used to swell up . . . the doctor said we were fed too much and so on odd days mother missed a slice . . . on those days I used to hide on an empty lot in back of a bakery . . . my brothers and sisters never looked for me . . . I would sniff the odors coming through the windows of the bakery, but odors don't even puff up the belly. . . . [*Pause.*] I decided to

have no children when I grew up . . . and I laughed
then . . . now I do not laugh at it anymore. . . .

GITEL

It would be against our dreams to let the blind
multiply, while we who see fade away without leav-
ing a shadow to complete our dreams. . . .

> [YANKEL'S *wedding:* BEGGARS *are at the doors*
> *. . . musicians are playing softly . . . hum*
> *and bustle . . . the music plays on . . . the*
> *light of dawn steals upon the scene . . .*
> *the wedding music gallops over buildings,*
> *fire escapes, sleeping people.*]
>
> *In a Hall*

MASTER OF CEREMONIES

A speech from the bride's father! Berel Diamond
. . . the bride's father, is going to say a few words!

BEREL

I want to say a few words to my future son-in-law
and my daughter and to all the young people present. I made good in America! I made money! I
saw the opportunity and I worked as hard as I
could. That's why I don't have to work any more
now . . . my children have everything they want
. . . one of them is a judge . . . the other a doctor
and, as you see, my daughter is marrying a fine man

tonight—a leader of men, who is honored by everybody!

THE GUESTS

Bravo! Bravo! Bravo!

BEREL

Peace has come to me!
[*Two* PEDDLERS, *carrying bundles, walk in*]

MASTER OF CEREMONIES

And here are representatives of the Peddlers As-
sociation who wish to honor the bridegroom and
present him with handsome presents.

FIRST PEDDLER

To our leader and honored neighbor: Mazol Tov!

SECOND PEDDLER

Joy and happiness to you and your future wife
and children!

YANKEL

You people who have helped me become a respected leader of this ward, I want to say to you
that I thank you and if actions speak louder than
words, I can say to you, that from now on you can
peddle on this street. Now that the gangster
Yoshke is put away from us for good, you can have

freedom and peace. Of course, you must obey the laws and support the organization which gives you that freedom. Once you get a license, it'll be good until revoked! Drinks and cake for my honored guests!

[*He shakes hands with the* PEDDLERS.]

THE GUESTS

Bravo! Bravo! Bravo!

THE MASTER OF CEREMONIES

Music! Music! Let the music stop! I want to say that this is the finest wedding I've ever been to. Music! Music. Let the music start! And now I'll say a few words for Rebe Shlome Finkel, the bridegroom's father, who is so happy that he can't speak for himself. . . . [*Laughter.*] He is a fine man and a great scholar who became a great merchant in America through hard labor and honesty! Three cheers for Reb Shlome! Hooray! Hooray! Hooray!

THE GUESTS

Hooray! Hooray! Hooray!

MASTER OF CEREMONIES

And here is a landsman who is bringing good wishes to the bride and bridegroom and also presents a silver tea set: Mr. and Mrs. Harris! And here is a couple well known to you all as two doves, who bring a well chosen present: a carving set! Let us hope the newly married couple will have something to carve! Mr. and Mrs. Bennie Goldstein! And here is a couple that's as popular as a breeze on a hot day, presenting to the happy couple a set of dishes! Mr. and Mrs. Isaac Golubov! The bridegroom's father presents to the couple a house full of furniture, and the bride's parents, besides the dowry, which is a sum no ten or fifteen or a hundred poor could afford, make a present of linen for the table and bed, and I shall present the bridegroom with my best wishes, being a poor man, and the bride with my blessing and a kiss! [*Moves to the bride. Suddenly newsboys dash on.*]

NEWSBOYS

Extra! Extra! Louis the Snipe goes to the electric chair! Electric chair! East side boy . . . extra!

> [*Run off . . . there is a slight stir, but the* MASTER OF CEREMONIES *covers it immediately.*]

MASTER OF CEREMONIES

Music! Music! Music! Dance! Dance! Dance! [*The musicians play a lively dance in which the*

older people take part . . . the beggars react to
this dance: right shoulder arm resting at cheek
bone . . . the hand and arm outstretched straight be-
fore them . . . head reclines to right . . . left foot
moves from heel up to toe, then to toe of right foot
. . . then down to heel of same foot remaining in
same place all the time. . . . VLADISLAV, *dressed in*
his best clothes, stands in his basement waiting for an
invitation . . . the dance keeps on . . . then as the
older people tire, drinks are served. . . .]
                                        In Headquarters

REUBEN

Do you hear the dance music?

GITEL

The death dance. . . . Louis the Snipe, is going
to the electric chair. . . . The East side has lost
a son . . . my brother is dancing. . . . My brother's
feet touch the ground. . . . Louis has no feet . . .
they belong to my brother . . . come let us dance
. . . tomorrow I shall make fifty shirtwaists for the
daughters of hell and heaven . . . the needle comes
down five hundred times a minute and I have nine
fingers left . . . let us dance.

    [*They dance . . . the guests at* YANKEL'S *wed-*
      ding also dance.]

Let us dance, Reuben. . . . We have feet . . . faster

. . . we have not been judged yet . . . faster! Faster! Faster!

[GITEL *and* REUBEN *embrace.*]

REUBEN

Listen! [*Pause.*] Do you hear voices . . . many voices? . . .

GITEL

[*In a hushed tone.*] Yes . . . where do they come from?

REUBEN

Do you hear . . . the earth trembling? . . .

GITEL

[*As before.*] Yes . . . what is that?

REUBEN

We are singing. . . .

GITEL

We are singing. . . .

REUBEN

Yes . . . we are marching and singing . . . we are shirtwaist workers . . . we are coolies in the rice fields . . . we are on a rubber plantation in Liberia . . . coal miners in Colorado . . . oil well drillers in Baku . . . we are the world . . . our song is one of triumph . . . our step gay. . . .

GITEL

We are marching . . . we are singing. . . .

REUBEN

Yes, we. . . .

GITEL

Over the ruins of Ghettoes . . . over the wastes of gangsters . . . of Rabbis we are marching . . . do you feel the light?

REUBEN

YES!

GITEL

It is not too strong for you?

REUBEN

No! I can see far away . . . far away. . . . I can see the world, the whole world!

GITEL

We are singing. . . .

REUBEN

We are marching. . . .

On the Stairs

[*The* FIRST *and* SECOND WOMEN *stick their heads out of somewhere simultaneously.*]

FIRST WOMAN

Mrs. Gold, Mrs. Gold, you hear me . . . you
. . . zzzzz.

SECOND WOMAN

Yes, yes, I was just going to call you! zzzzz.

FIRST WOMAN

Well, didn't I say to you that the strike will
soon be over and we'll be all right again? Do you
know what? I am moving! Yes! zzz.

SECOND WOMAN

Where? zzz.

FIRST WOMAN

To Harlem! zzz.

RABBI

To Harlem! zzz.

FIRST WOMAN

A gas range bath second floor three rooms rear
hot water two blocks from school and what are you
going to do?

SECOND WOMAN

We are moving, too, but not so far away . . .
to Delancey.

RABBI

Delancey.

FIRST WOMAN

It's all right . . . it's moving anyway, isn't it?
As long as we get away from here. And what do
you think of my next door? Moving to the Avenue!

SECOND WOMAN

What Avenue?

FIRST WOMAN

Second Avenue!

RABBI

Second Avenue.

SECOND WOMAN

But the big news is that Mrs. Boriskin is moving
to the Bronx!

FIRST WOMAN

Yes? You don't mean it! To the Bronx! OHO!
Everybody is moving . . . everybody . . . when are
you moving?

SECOND WOMAN

Right away! Why wait? . . . The moving men
ought to be here any minute . . . we are all packed
up . . . do you know what happened? My fingers
were wet and I broke the big glass pitcher with
the flowers on it . . . to pieces . . . what do you
think of that?

FIRST WOMAN

So, so . . . too bad . . . so she is moving to the Bronx. . . .

SECOND WOMAN

Someday we'll move to the Bronx too! Wait and see! I got to go in.

FIRST WOMAN

I got to finish my packing. . . . [*They go in.*]

On the Street

RABBI

Where shall I pray tonight? To the Bronx! I'll move, too! To the Bronx! That's where god is now! God has moved to the Bronx.

CHONO

[*Shakes* Zwi.] Ha? Ha? What's this? Ha? [*Starts up and tries to lift* Zwi,s *body—steps away.*] Forgive me! Forgive me, Zwi! You can sleep wherever you want to! Who is going to bury you, Zwi? Who is going to say Kadish after you? Who, Zwi, who? [*Takes out tin cup.*] Chdoko tachil mmoves! Chdoko tachil mmoves! They won't give you anything while you are alive; why should they give you alms when you are dead! [*He looks at* Zwi . . . *his eyes light on the shoes.*] Forgive me, Zwi, Zwi, forgive me and plead for me

when you go up into the clouds . . . forgive me
but 1 have to do this. . . . [*Takes off* Zwi's *shoes
and dangles them in the air.*] Shoes without laces
size nine, shoes without laces size nine, shoes without laces size nine. . . .

THE MACHINES

Whirrr . . . whirr. . . .

RABBI

To the Bronx! To the Bronx! To the Bronx!

FIRST PEDDLER

Here hereheherehere!

SECOND PEDDLER

Just two left, just two, just two!

THIRD PEDDLER

I'm losing money! I'm losing money! I'm losing
money!

THE PEDDLERS

Here, here, here, one more left, one more hereher-
hereherherehere!

[THE SHAMES *appears with a big sign: "Apart-
ment house going up on this site. Three
rooms sixty dollars." He hangs it on the*

*wall of one of the tenements. Wreckers with
picks and shovels begin tearing down the
building . . . moving men carry out furniture
and household goods.*]

THE MACHINES

Whirrr . . . whirrrrrrrrr . . . whirrrrrrrrrr.

THE PEDDLERS

Whohehahenooononononherehere last one, last one,
last one, last, no more left, no more!

THE MACHINES

Whirrrr . . . whirrrrrr . . . whirrrrrrrrr. . . .

CHONO

Shoes without laces size nine!
   [*The women are saying farewell to each other.
   The machines throttle the air pockets. . . .*]

RABBI

To the Bronx!

THE MACHINES

Whirrrrr . . . whirrrrrr . . . whirrrrrr. . . .

VLADISLAV

Someday I go away. . . .
   [*But no one can hear his voice, for* THE PED-

DLERS *are shouting again . . . the* RABBI *is
singing on . . . Chono is selling the shoes
. . . the wreckers are smashing the building and*]

THE CURTAINS CLOSE